TE@CHER TOOLKIT

Bloomsbury Education
An imprint of Bloomsbury Publishing Plc

50 Bedford Square
London
WC1B 3DP
UK

1385 Broadway
New York
NY 10018
USA

www.bloomsbury.com

Bloomsbury is a registered trade mark of Bloomsbury Publishing Plc

First published 2015

British Library Cataloguing-in-Publication Data
A catalogue record for this book is available from the British Library.

ISBN:
HB 9781472929815
PB 9781472910844
ePub 9781472910851
ePDF 9781472910868

Library of Congress Cataloging-in-Publication Data

A catalog record for this book is available from the Library of Congress.

10 9 8 7 6 5 4 3 2 1

Design by Marcus Duck Design
Cover illustration (and Vitruvian teacher throughout the book) © Jean Julien
Illustrations © Polly Norton
Printed and bound by CPI Group (UK) Ltd, Croydon CR0 4YY

This book is produced using paper that is made from wood grown in managed, sustainable forests. It is natural, renewable and recyclable. The logging and manufacturing processes conform to the environmental regulations of the country of origin.

To view more of our titles please visit www.bloomsbury.com

Every effort has been made to trace the copyright holders and to obtain permission for use of copyright material. The author and publishers would be pleased to rectify any error or omission in future editions.

Quotes from government documents used in this publication are approved under an Open Government Licence: www.nationalarchives.gov.uk/doc/open-government-licence/version/3/

TE@CHER TOOLKIT

ROSS MORRISON McGILL

Helping you survive your first five years

ACKNOWLEDGEMENTS

Thank you to the following people for their contributions:

Amjad Ali, Alex Atherton, Shawki Bakkar, John Bayley, Jill Berry, Roy Blatchford, Rob Campbell, Sue Cowley, Paul Dix, Cherryl Drabble, Stephen Drew, Nancy Gedge, Sapuran Gill, Tracey Griffiths, Beth Kelly, Debra Kidd, Jackson Ogunyemi, Matt O'Leary, Jane Manzone, Peps McCrea, Tom Sherrington, Benita Simmons, Rehana Shanks, Paul Sutton, David Weston and @DisIdealist.

Download the 5 minute lesson plans found in this book from my blog!
teachertoolkit.me/vitruvianteaching

Dedication

This is an unusual opportunity to share one of my father's 'best-design-ideas-yet-to-reach-the-market' before you start reading this book. 'Ross, floating soap! Place an air pocket inside the soap; perfect for bath time; or, place the soap inside a sponge and have constant lather. Floating soap: see. I told you!'

This is one product only Loughborough University were allowed to see in 1992. Sadly, I didn't get the A-level grades to make it to be a designer, but instead, headed off to Goldsmiths College to become the teacher I am today. It was the best rejection I ever had.

Thank you dad.

I dedicate the bones of this book to the two people whom it would not have been possible to do without; my wife and all the support she has given me – she has the patience of a saint – and to my son who, after hours of writing, pulled me away from the desk when I have most needed a 'bundle' or a race up and down the garden!

Thank you for allowing me to write this book.

THANK YOUS

I would like to give an almighty 'high-five' to **Holly Gardner** for her patience and persistence in helping me to complete this book. We did it Holly! And to **Emily Wilson** for her invaluable and astute editorial skills!

To the marvellous **Marcus Duck** who has designed the book layouts and to **Jean Julien** for his front cover illustration of the Vitruvian teacher and the translation of my book concept for teachers moving towards Vitruvian teaching: what a great image!

The biggest thank you goes to ex-student **Polly Norton**, for her creativity and for going along with my 'teaching ideas'; and despite sketching outside of her comfort zone, has stuck to her own ideology and has intertwined her brilliant illustrations with my classroom anecdotes. Her artwork is superb. Please do follow this up-and-coming artist on Twitter at @PollyNor.

Thank you to headteachers past and present, who have been a constant source of support and inspiration over the past two decades; you know who you are. I'd also like to provide an acknowledgment to **Stephen Tierney** and to **Mark Healy**, who've always been on the phone for me, offering humour and wisdom throughout my journey.

This book is for every teacher who has been bullied; those forced to take redundancy and for the thousands of teachers who leave the profession within the first five years. Hopefully, this book may entice you back into the classroom!

Everyone is born equal; then some become teachers!

Ross Morrison McGill
@TeacherToolkit

INTRODUCING THE VITRUVIAN TEACHER

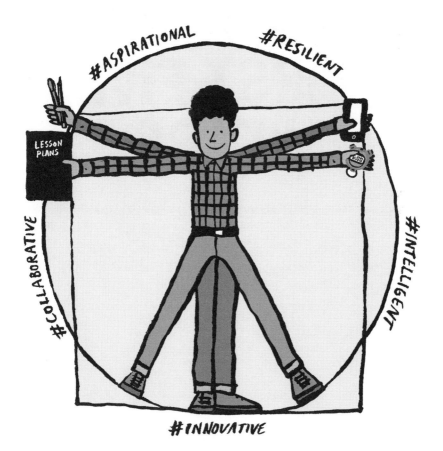

VITRUVIAN TEACHING WILL HELP YOU TO SURVIVE YOUR FIRST FIVE YEARS

The Vitruvian teacher is...

1. RESILIENT

2. INTELLIGENT

3. INNOVATIVE

4. COLLABORATIVE

5. ASPIRATIONAL

Start working towards Vitruvian today!

INTRODUCTION

Being a teacher is a demanding job, yet it is one in which you can essentially change people's lives! I went into teaching knowing that I wanted to be a teacher: a teacher who could make a real difference to the lives of others.

WHERE I STARTED

I am one of four sons, brought up by devout religious parents who were officers (religious ministers) of The Salvation Army. We shared our day-to-day living quarters with those less fortunate than ourselves, so after school I was sometimes found alongside drug addicts; alcoholics; schizophrenics and delinquents sizing up the 8-ball at the end of a pool cue! My family travelled from job to job all over the UK and as a consequence, my schooling was sporadic. From the age of five, the longest time we stayed in one place was three years and this was towards the end of my school career. It was too little too late – the damage had already been done! I did not excel at school, failing to gain good grades in almost all subjects. Yet my experiences of failure in school, shaped the teacher I have become today.

My first formal experience of teaching came at the age of 19 when I started a teacher training degree. As a child, my father had always encouraged me to generate new ideas on paper and in conversation and his passion for gizmos and gadgets enraptured me for days on end. Design was a very natural field for me so teaching design seemed like the ideal choice. Looking back, I can see that this is where my love for creativity and generating new ideas was born. It was the beginning of *@TeacherToolkit* and I didn't even know it!

WHAT MAKES A GOOD TEACHER?

#RESILIENT

Call me old-fashioned, but I like hard work! Teaching, learning and the world of education are my life blood. My father was my motivation and still is. There is no doubt that teaching was challenging when I first qualified but it's even more stressful, complicated and regulated today. It's incredibly hard now for those new to the profession to stay longer than five years in the classroom, yet I believe teaching is more rewarding than ever before! In this book I share my classroom ups and downs and offer advice so that you can learn from my successes (and mistakes) and come out the other side.

#INTE

So, what makes a good teacher?

As teachers, values and vision will play a vital role in growing and defining our own pedagogy. If you shed all the external distractions such as lesson planning, accountability, marking and all the other constituents that we encounter in teaching, you are left with pedagogy. The 'what, why and how' we do what we do in the classroom – your vision and values. The key difference between your values and a vision for teaching is this. Vision can only be applicable to you in your own school. Values are what belong to you and dictate how you live your life. Values will evolve according to your own experiences; the demographics of where you live; the psychographics of you (and your family) and so forth… The circumstances that shaped you as a trainee teacher will also define your own values within a school. The experiences you have within each department and within each school you work in will help to define your values too. Along our professional journey, we will be dealt a set of cards that we must learn to use to our advantage. Situations and experiences in our personal lives will influence our decisions and values. We are all born with a genetic code and as teachers we have the capacity to shape it further into our very own 'teacher genetic code'.

If I could offer the reader a conclusion at the beginning of this book rather than at the end, it would be:

There is no single way to become a great teacher.

The perfect teacher does NOT exist, nor am I suggesting that he/she ever has done, or that this accolade is achievable from reading this, or in fact any book! Instead, you will find my lifetime's craft to date, distilled into a few hundred pages of text so you can have to hand all my little gems of advice and hardboiled experience to reference in a pragmatic way. You can try out whatever strategy you choose, in your own classroom in your very next lesson! **TE@CHER TOOLKIT** for me is my 'teaching soul' poured out. I have delved deep into my past and have imparted as much as I can physically and mentally muster into this single manuscript.

There is NO silver bullet in this book that will cure any personal weakness in your own teaching. Education is a lifelong journey and this book serves merely as another chapter in your own professional learning journey. This is my story that I would like you to be part of.

HOW WILL THIS BOOK HELP ME?

TE@CHER TOOLKIT will provide you with a carefully selected range of strategies and thoughts based on my two decades in the classroom. I share my experiences of classroom observations, meetings, lesson planning, marking, behaviour management, having a form group, running assemblies, sharing resources, working with TAs – you name it, I have done it and share it with you in these pages. There are ups and there are downs. And I'll share the secret of the glower with you…

In addition to this I have included four of my 5 minute lesson plans, one of which is brand new, never seen before! Turn the pages to find it now.

WHO IS THIS BOOK FOR?

TE@CHER TOOLKIT is for those currently in teacher training, those teachers who are new to the classroom and to those working towards or approaching that elusive fifth year of teaching. In this book, I refer to the 40% attrition rate (DfE) in England and suggest an armful of strategies for how you can get build strong foundations and survive when the going gets tough.

Throughout all my years in the classroom things have never been tougher than in my first five years, but don't be disheartened! There have been some easy times, but there have also been many, many moments when I've wanted to leave the profession. In this book, I share with you what's kept me in the classroom all this time and why I still believe teaching is a lifelong vocation. I offer anecdotes from colleagues that will provide you with the context, relationships and strategies for working and staying put in the classroom; to not only survive your first five years but to help you thrive for a lifetime!

No matter how hard you look, you will find NO mention of the word 'Ofsted' in this book, other than in this sentence! From now on, this watchdog will be referred to by my preferred nickname: the 'Grim Reaper'! I strongly believe the watchdog will eventually cease to exist in its current form.

WHY THE VITRUVIAN TEACHER?

When thinking about writing this book, I thought about the journey I first took and about the countless teachers I have mentored into the profession along the way. I worked through in detail, every aspect of school life from trainee, to that first set of school responsibilities that are given on the cusp of middle leadership. I reflected on an article I wrote about the 'Visual Anatomy of a Great Teacher' and an analogy I made with Leonardo Da Vinci's 'Vitruvian Man'. Vitruvius was most famous for his work called *De architectura* consisting of ten books on architecture written between 20-30 BC. 'Vitruvius believed that an architect should focus on three central themes when preparing a design for a building: firmitas (strength), utilitas (functionality), and venustas (beauty)' and he made links to the human body and its 'ideal proportions' (British Library).

I adapted this philosophy into what I believe to be the qualities needed in the first five years of every teachers' journey. I broke each year into five qualities: Resilient, Intelligent, Innovative, Collaborative and Aspirational. **TE@CHER TOOLKIT** is a compendium of everything you need to know linked to these five qualities which I believe will help you to develop and survive your first five years.

- **RESILIENT** Year 1 – surviving your NQT year
- **INTELLIGENCE** Year 2 – refining your teaching
- **INNOVATIVE** Year 3 – take risks and be creative
- **COLLABORATIVE** Year 4 – share and work with others
- **ASPIRATIONAL** Year 5 – moving towards middle leadership

GET STARTED NOW!

When you complete your teacher training you are not the finished product – you are always 'in training'. Teaching is a vocation and you have only just been cast into a template to begin surviving and thriving. Your journey is far from begun. After all my time in the classroom, I am not the finished article either! I am not the same teacher I am today, that I was 20 years ago, last year or even last term. I am always evolving, regardless of fad or fashion, goalpost or policy. I adapt to meet the needs of my students and my school.

Throughout your career, you will gain knowledge, skill and experience, but nothing quite matches the reality of being in the classroom. All these parts of your repertoire must be connected to make up the greater whole; you must be made of the right character and fit together by your own definition. This is what I call the Vitruvian Teacher. Start working towards Vitruvian today.

1
RESILIENT

'One of my most memorable experiences
as a newly qualified teacher was marking
in my broom cupboard... It was the perfect
cubbyhole for marking – and taking a nap!'

BE RESILIENT

You're anxious and feeling isolated; you know that your students are starting to dictate the tempo of the lesson rather than you, and that two or three key players are setting the tone. Sooner, rather than later, even the well-behaved kids are going to follow suit. What next?

Most newly qualified and beginning teachers will be able to say what to do next in theory, but actually putting it into practice in the classroom is a lot more difficult! No matter what you do, in your first years as a teacher you'll come across situations like this. You'll never quite feel like you're finished. You will also always think that you could have done better, or that someone else might have done it another way!*

Until you master the classroom, sadly these realities will eat into your personal life, and continue to ebb into your thinking unless you secure the ultimate classroom basics. For me, the key to your first year of teaching is RESILIENCE.

You are right. Your work will never be done and it can always be done a different way!

WHAT IS RESILIENCE?

The definition of resilience is: 'able to withstand or recover quickly from difficult conditions'.

Being resilient requires you to be **stable**, **strong**, **hard-wearing**, **determined** and **steadfast**. It is a daily necessity and a mindset to constantly strive for in your first year of teaching, and indeed your first five years and beyond.

Resilience is not a quality you are born with. And I personally believe you cannot teach it directly. We have to learn to be resilient as a direct result of our ability – or inability – to overcome major difficulties in our own personal or professional lives. We must learn from our mistakes, each time growing stronger and stronger, and being better prepared for the next time we encounter anything that is difficult. We therefore learn to be resilient when faced with challenging situations. And this, I maintain, is a

key attribute for surviving the first year in teaching and for building the foundations of a strong teaching career.

WHY RESILIENCE?

If I think back over the 20 years I've been in the classroom, resilience – or staying strong – is the one key factor that can sum up my experience thus far. I've had countless setbacks, as you will too, but no more or less than most teachers. Through being resilient I have kept going! Believe me; I'm no hero and I am not unique. I have wanted to quit several times and at the start of section 3 I discuss an occasion when I have wanted to jump ship! But to me, teaching is all about allowing your experiences in life and in the classroom to shape you as a teacher. And when things go wrong, or not as you expected, you need to learn to be able to pick yourself up, carry on and learn from the setback.

I do not intend to fuzz over the details here. Teaching is an incredibly difficult and complex job to do. It was difficult way back in 1993 when I did my training, working on a blackboard with no computer or interactive whiteboard in sight! It is difficult today, with the increased pressures on teachers to meet examination targets and the increased burdens of accountability and workload, coupled with the pinch on wages and pensions and the increasing costs of living that have made living as a teacher financially very tough.

However, make no mistake about it, teaching is a lifetime vocation. I entered the profession for two very simple reasons: I loved my subject and I loved working with kids. It was a no-brainer. What brought you into teaching? What motivates you? (Please tell me it's not because of the school holidays!)

Resilient teachers can adapt to their strengths and cope with varying degrees of unpredictable circumstances in school. Teachers who lack resilience may be overwhelmed. (Warning: this will happen in your first year at least once.) Teachers who lack resilience dwell on obstacles

that hinder self-development. (Warning: this will also happen!) The nature of the profession requires us all to be reflective; a skill that once mastered, will be one of the keys to unlocking your levels of resilience.

Surviving the first five years of your teaching career is, for most, like riding a fairground attraction: tight turns; steep slopes; wild and unpredictable changes!

In teaching, we are, no matter what we may think, creatures of habit. Institutionalised by timetables; an hourly bell to tell us all when to move; school dinners; staffroom politics and teacher vs. student discussions and agreements (I'm the adult, you are the child – that sort of thing). But we also regularly encounter various experiences that challenge the norm.

In this section, I discuss resilience in all things teaching and all things teacher. I cover the main areas you need to get to grips with early on to develop resilient foundations on which to build your subsequent teaching career.

Twitter name: @TeacherToolkit

Name in real life: Ross Morrison McGill

What's his job? Deputy headteacher in London and prolific blogger

Specialist topic? Design technology, lesson planning

Why should I follow him? I am a classroom teacher who specialises in design technology and I have taught in the classroom since the age of 18. I have been a school leader since 2000 and started working as a deputy headteacher in September 2014. I write about education, focusing on teaching and learning and staff well-being, and I create and share classroom resources online. This has evolved into writing more and more about school leadership, staff development and educational policy, particularly challenging the ivory towers.

MEET & TWEET

MARK, PLAN, TEACH, REPEAT!

Great teaching isn't complicated – it's about getting the simple things right. This is a mantra of mine that I have developed over the years, and it's a really important one for you to keep in mind, especially in your first few years of teaching. Some of the 'simple things' you need to get on top of as soon as you can in year one will be to secure good marking, good planning and good teaching.

1. MARK ➡ 2. PLAN ➡ 3. TEACH
REPEAT

Throughout your teaching career, you will always need to mark, plan and teach. Always! Getting these elements right will take time, especially the 'teach' part, and unfortunately all three will consume your every waking (and sometimes sleeping) minute in and out of school until you can develop a skill set for reducing the time you take to address at least two of the fundamental basics: marking and planning.

Let's look in more detail at the three very humble expectations of every teacher.

1. **Mark** Mark your books! You will be bombarded with marking. You will bury your head in the sand. You will work late into the night. You will ask yourself, 'Why did I bother?' when students discard the marking you have provided for them, or when the vast majority of students don't actually act on the feedback you have given to them. But I repeat, mark your books regardless. (See pages 7–11 for how to mark meaningfully without it consuming your life.)

2. **Plan** Love it or hate it, your teacher training will instil into your being the need to plan lessons well. Some will dictate that the more detailed the lesson plan, the better your lesson will be – which is absolute nonsense! There is a lot of value in lesson planning, however, and I still believe that even after a long stint in the classroom it does serve a very important purpose for you and your students; but it should not impact on you and your well-being every single day. (See pages 12–17 for smarter planning advice.)

3. **Teach** The third humble expectation of every teacher is to teach well. You must mark your books and plan lessons so you can teach well. This is not something that you should aim to achieve straight away. Your teaching will improve over time, and this whole book is aimed at helping you continue to improve.

I want to make sure that you have really understood how important these three elements are for building resilient foundations in your first year, and hopefully for many more years to come. Here is the process again:

1. MARK — You may think it strange that this cycle starts with marking, but your marking will and should inform all your lesson plans. Reading your students' work and getting to grips with their individual level of understanding and anything they have misunderstood is invaluable for getting your plan right for the next lesson.

2. PLAN — Plan in whatever form works for you. Use the 5 minute lesson plan before you teach (see page 15) or create a detailed step by step programme of everything you want to cover… Just make sure that you do it, and that it's informed by the people it matters to most – the students you are teaching.

3. TEACH — Teach what you have planned, or don't if your class leads the lesson somewhere else more interesting – but try to love it, breathe it, share it and get better at it. Go with the flow and take risks!

REPEAT — Yes – now do it all again! A little bit better than last time (probably).

RESILIENCE TIP

Do expect disasters! We have all had them and I will most likely have another soon enough. So, plan B must always be at the back of your mind when teaching (and planning). The odd thing about teaching is that you can expect planned lessons to go down the pan, and others that you have not planned for to go marvellously well. Why? Students can be unpredictable, so can your lesson planning and so can your teaching. But, have you actually stopped to think about why some lessons are successful and others not so successful? Try and do this as much as you can.

MARK

I have to confess that I once paid my sister-in-law to mark some of my exam papers. There was a simple assessment criteria, so all in all, very straightforward. I was very young and incredibly exhausted.

Was this a good idea and worth the time saved (and the money spent)?

Absolutely not. I had to go through all the exam papers at a later date anyway to ensure that I could give precise feedback to each child. (I'd be lying if I didn't admit that it did feel worth it at the time – just for a short while.)

When it comes to marking, you will pull your hair out trying to discover strategies that work best for you and your students. You will try to cut down the time taken; you may even get students to mark the books for themselves (this is OK!). And no doubt over your years of teaching, you will leave a pile of marking in the corner of your classroom and will take the occasional guilty look over at the reams of paper and books gathering dust, and promise yourself that you **will** actually have some more time tomorrow to do it, just not right *now*!

When looking at that pile of marking, you will probably consider the following:

- Can I get away with not marking this work at all?

- If so, for how long?

- Could I mark them in one of my non-contact lessons at school, rather than at home during my own time?

- When is the next departmental book scrutiny? (Great, no book-looks soon!)

- If I don't mark the work, will so-and-so ask for their book?

- Could I just leave them in the corner and forget they are there?

- Will my conscience learn to live with my decision?

- Will the students even read my feedback anyway?

I vividly recall the time when I allowed 30 pieces of homework to fall slowly out of the palm of my hands – into a recycling bin. (I know! Forgive me.) This is utterly reprehensible, but proved a very valuable lesson indeed…

Three months later. Parents' evening… Scenario: poker face!

Some teachers will want to (and do) mark everything. But, each time a student submits a piece of work, *not* every single piece of work should be, or can be, marked. You will question school expectations when they do not meet your own departmental views, or even your own individual interpretations of assessment.

You will question why some students leave your feedback on the floor, and so you should. But, just remember – you cannot mark everything. Don't expect that you can maintain this, and don't even try. You **must** be in a position where you want to mark students' books… but not every single piece of work. Plan to work smarter.

I do wish that I had known this all those years ago when I allowed those pieces of paper to slip guiltily from my hands.

TYPES OF MARKING

Marking falls into two categories:

1. SUMMATIVE MARKING

Summative marking is marking a piece of work according to a framework or success criteria, and giving it a grade. **Summative = to assess.**

The key questions to ask yourself when it comes to summative marking are:

- Does the school, department or Key Stage have an agreed system for teachers to use?

- What grading system are you going to use?

- Are you going to use GCSE or A-level grades?

- Is it a numerical mark out of 10 or 20?

WHAT WOULD YOU DO?
Tweet me @TeacherToolkit

2. FORMATIVE MARKING

Formative marking is not about giving a grade, but rather providing commentary on the level the student is working at in order to improve learning.
Formative = to inform.

Think about the following when it comes to formative marking:

- **Comment system** Do you have an agreed way of making comments on students' work that all your students understand? Is there an agreed marking code? Try some of the following:

  - WWW (What went well…)
  - EBI (Even better if…)
  - IOTI (In order to improve…)
  - Three stars and a wish

- **Numbers or letters for key marking points** Have you considered compiling a list of key marking points for the students and assigning each point a number or letter? That way you can give comments via the numbers or letters instead of writing the comments out in full. How about annotating the piece of work by putting the numbers/letters against the corresponding questions or text?

- **Time for corrections** Once you've spent time putting comments on students' work, they must go back and either correct errors or redo areas of their work that need improvement. A good strategy is to give students time to correct or redo the work during the lesson as soon as you hand it back to them. This is a key part of them improving and learning from past mistakes.

Turn to page 10 to find the 5 minute marking plan!

Some of the places I have marked and my judgements on their reliability

Bad

1. **The garden** Not a very reliable place in the winter, and considering you only have one or two months in term time throughout the year with viable access to the outdoors, marking in the garden is a total fantasy. Avoid at all costs; you are only kidding yourself.

2. **The pub** Poor results, often decreasing in reliability as time/liquid consumption goes on.

3. **The bus** Perfect for assessing visual work, but terrible reliability for proofreading and red pen accuracy.

4. **The classroom** Pretty reliable – you don't need to take the work home and you have the resources around you to assist with the process. One huge flaw though, is that a colleague could walk in on you and say absolutely anything that can make or break your mojo, for example: 'This work/assessment is amazing! Can I have a copy?' Or: 'Can I borrow you for a minute?' *Heart sinks*

5. **Another office away from your department** Often a good strategy if you want to get away from colleagues who are chatting in your space. The down side is, a strange face in another part of a large secondary school can attract even more chatter.

6. **The staffroom** Staffrooms will vary significantly from school to school; from underused to overused, from no table space and not enough computer access, to plenty of areas to work in. Make an assessment about whether yours is a reliable working environment

7. **The departmental office** A very reliable place to work. Often a safe haven. You'll know your colleagues well and there will be unwritten rules about when to work, when to ask for advice, when to speak, when not to speak, when to laugh, when to cry... and when to mark!

8. **The kitchen table** A very reliable solution. With non-lyrical music on the radio, perhaps a favourite tipple and a reward promised at the end – such as a night at the pub, a takeaway or evening dinner – it's probably my favourite place for marking, and the most effective.

9. **The departmental broom cupboard** One of my most memorable experiences as a newly qualified teacher was marking in my broom cupboard, exit stage right of my classroom. It was a small tool cupboard, big enough for a handful of textbooks, scalpels, chisels, reserve packets of pencils and crisps... You name it, I had it in this cupboard. It was the perfect cubbyhole for marking – and taking a nap!

Good

5 MINUTE MARKING PLAN

...photocopy or download, and scribble your way to focusing on student assessment!

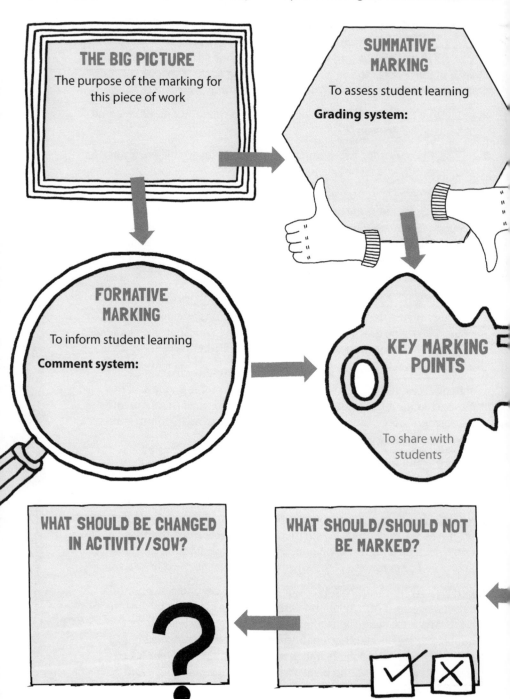

THE BIG PICTURE

The purpose of the marking for this piece of work

SUMMATIVE MARKING

To assess student learning

Grading system:

FORMATIVE MARKING

To inform student learning

Comment system:

KEY MARKING POINTS

To share with students

WHAT SHOULD BE CHANGED IN ACTIVITY/SOW?

WHAT SHOULD/SHOULD NOT BE MARKED?

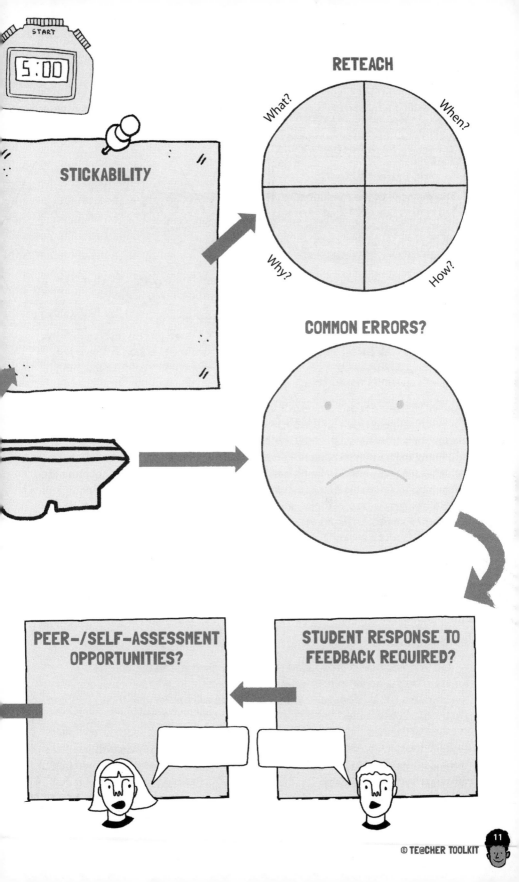

PLAN

The second expectation of every teacher worldwide is this: to plan lessons. Whether this is mentally or on a piece of paper, lesson by lesson or over a longer period of time – you choose what works best for you.

SHOULD YOU PREPARE DETAILED LESSON PLANS?

The level of detail required in a lesson plan as stipulated by your teacher training institution is not manageable long term, but is important to begin with.

You will be compensated with extra time to do this planning during your PGCE year, and less time during your NQT year. There is a need for this level of detail at this stage in your career. Why? So that you can learn the required components of planning. But the lesson plan will never really match the reality of teaching it. Always keep this in mind. Always have a plan B.

As an NQT, the laborious process of lesson planning is very important, whether this is scribbling an idea on the back of a piece of paper or using your teacher planner or school template. I say this because I am 20 years down the road and know that my lesson planning was key to my students reaching their full potential. At times I had to be resilient, and over time I learnt that if I commanded 'stickability' (i.e. what learning is going to stick and be taken away, see page 15), I could have my lesson planning focused solely on the students' learning. If, as a young 23-year-old, I'd had the vantage point I have today, I would not have struggled as much as I did.

So often as new teachers, we lesson plan to control student behaviour, focusing on activities or exciting ideas that we intend (or hope) will make a difference to how they behave in that lesson. But, you and I both know that students are complicated individuals and that all teachers need to have high expectations of them and be incredibly organised and reflective from lesson to lesson so that they can break down barriers and be able to impart their subject knowledge.

Where so many others have failed when it comes to lesson planning is in focusing on the actual activity rather than the learning. We plan what activity the students will be doing and what activity we will be doing at the same time. We then become fixated on the fact that students are not cutting out pieces of paper in the specific way required or at the specific time allocated, and over the last decade – particularly in graded lesson observations – teachers have been branded failures because they have not stuck to the lesson plan and have deviated from the structure.

SHOULD YOU PREPARE 'LEAN' LESSON PLANS?

Do not let schools, mentors or HET (Higher Education Institute) providers stipulate that you 'must' produce lesson plans. I will (and did on the previous page) insist that as a new teacher you will need to go through this process in order to understand what fragments of learning you need to facilitate for your students. But what purpose does it serve you and your school to maintain this – whether you are an all-singing, all-dancing teacher; a maverick; a veteran; or someone who has been told you are below par? Meticulous lesson planning is **not** needed.

Lesson by lesson, or perhaps day-to-day, planning becomes less significant as your experience grows. Your resilience develops in order to manage day-to-day teaching. As you take on extra responsibilities and understand the nature of the academic year, you recognise pivotal points in the year where lesson planning is not so crucial. Over time, experience kicks in and if you 'start with the end in mind', this habit will have more impact than laborious lesson planning.

A scheme of work over the course of the term will give you a clear indication of the route you want to take your students on in order to be successful in your subject. Having an 'overall big picture' as you gather teaching experience will therefore reduce the need for a 'day-to-day big picture' and pedantic lesson plans.

RESILIENCE TIP

To be truly resilient, all teachers need to move towards a model of medium-term planning so that lesson planning is lean on content, yet rich and full of cognition. This is the 'why'. What are we learning and why? If you can move towards a model of lesson planning that focuses on 'what are we learning' rather than 'what are we doing', you will soon develop a level of confidence in your own lesson planning that focuses on what is important in your teaching; progress over time rather than viewing individual lessons as standalone activities. 'Assess what is working and what is not in your classroom.' (@pepsmccrea)

See page 18 for more information on @pepsmccrea.

THE ULTIMATE GUIDE TO LESSON PLANNING

Whether you choose to plan your lessons one at a time, week by week or not at all, this is my ultimate guide to what you need in every lesson plan. The list below is a suggestion. It is not a definitive list. It is not how to deliver an outstanding lesson (or an inadequate one, for that matter!), it's simply what I do and what works for me. It should serve as a useful reminder and offer some key lesson planning headlines.

- **The big picture** Always have the big picture in mind. This is the context of your class (what stage the students are at), the interventions that you have planned and the resources that you need. Start with the end goal in mind.

- **Objectives and success criteria** Always plan to have an objective for the lesson or sequence of lessons. Don't keep this to yourself; share the success criteria with the students. I'm really bad at this and have to write a regular reminder to myself. I'm not keen on writing objectives on the board or asking students to record them in their books. In her book, *Notes from the Front Line* Debra Kidd (@debrakidd) warns: 'Even if, in every lesson, just two minutes are spent on [students copying objectives], that is 10 minutes per day, 50 minutes per week and 32.5 hours of learning lost per year.' Scrap copying them down, but make sure students understand the objective by sharing it verbally. It should never be left to guesswork.

- **Engagement** This is not always a requirement. Of the lessons I teach, 90% are dull as dishwater because in reality students are either working in silence, working independently, completing coursework, completing an assessment, revising or occasionally performing. To introduce key concepts, or what I want to call 'stickability', I plan for difficult concepts to be delivered through engagement. The engaging activity or anecdote is simply an ulterior motive, or a distraction to engage learners. In his book *Oops!*, Hywel Roberts (@HYWEL–ROBERTS) calls this 'the Hook'.

- **Stickability** This is very important. (See opposite).

- **Literacy/numeracy** Always plan to extrapolate something numerical or cover some literacy to help develop knowledge and skills.

- **Assessment for Learning** This is one of the most difficult parts of teaching: to plan for students to be able to self-assess and peer-assess each other's work. Make sure you communicate goals, feedback and summative points to enable students to make progress.

- **Differentiation** Differentiation is planning various techniques and resources to allow students to access the curriculum in your subject. This does not have to be planned for every individual lesson, but do plan for it over time.

- **Resources** Time-consuming, but essential. Beg, steal and borrow. Search for inspiration online. Maintain a stockpile, and keep it fresh.

- **Learning episodes** You dictate what will be teacher led and what will be student led. There is no expectation that any set number of episodes is anticipated in an individual lesson. You should decide what works best for you and your students, and be flexible. Forget progress shown in one lesson. It's a myth!

#stickability

Stickability is fundamental in every single lesson plan. You will hear me talk about it a lot. I am now at the stage where this simple component is all I consider. What are students learning? What will they take away? What will they bring back to class? That's it! Nail this and keep the learning focused on 'stickability'.

The 5 minute lesson plan

I first saw the 5 minute lesson plan in 2008. I first shared it in 2010. Since sharing it online, it has been:

- viewed over a million times!
- translated into 11 languages.
- downloaded in over 150 countries.

There are now 30 similar versions in the series that have been adapted by teachers the world over! There is also a digital version that converts plans into PDF files which is live and spreading rapidly online.

So if you haven't tried it, get planning now – it'll only take 5 minutes!

Have a look at the video tutorial for the 5 minute lesson plan here: ⟶

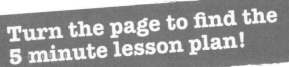

Turn the page to find the 5 minute lesson plan!

5 MINUTE LESSON PLAN

...photocopy or download, and scribble your way to smarter lesson planning!

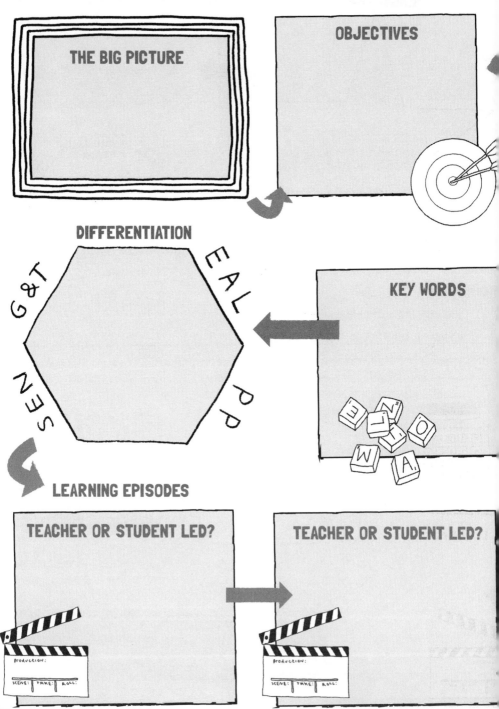

THE BIG PICTURE

OBJECTIVES

DIFFERENTIATION

G&T

EAL

SEN

PP

KEY WORDS

LEARNING EPISODES

TEACHER OR STUDENT LED?

TEACHER OR STUDENT LED?

PRODUCTION:
SCENE: TAKE: ROLL:

PRODUCTION:
SCENE: TAKE: ROLL:

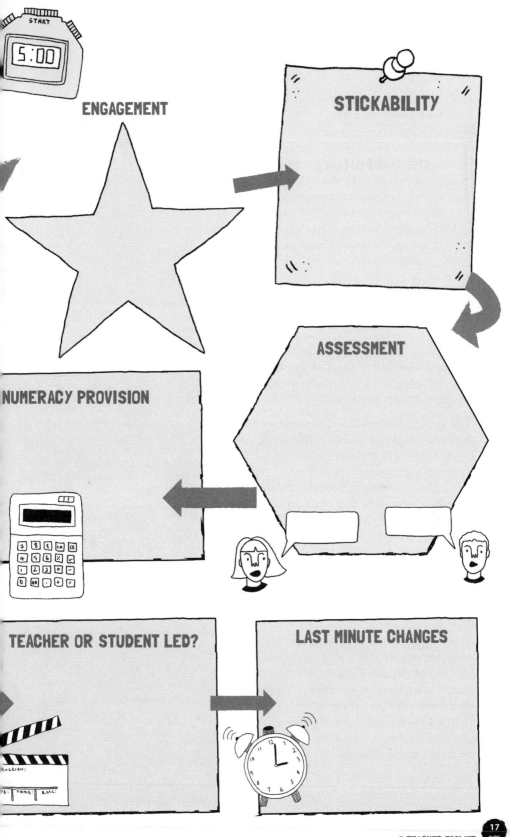

ENGAGEMENT

STICKABILITY

ASSESSMENT

NUMERACY PROVISION

TEACHER OR STUDENT LED?

LAST MINUTE CHANGES

5:00   START

TEACH

Mark, then plan… and then teach. You will start teaching in your first year but don't expect to be perfect in that year. The rest of this book will ask you to reflect on your teaching, and by the end of your first five years you will be much improved, but you will never be perfect; there is no such thing as 'the perfect teacher'. You will and should continue to improve by sharing, evaluating and reflecting on your teaching. Teaching is a lifetime's craft.

RESOURCES

Things that will help you with your teaching straight away and are key for your first five years are resources. Plan resources to help you teach!

As you start to learn how to manage your time you will create your own resources, but to begin with grab resources from wherever you can. Nab them from colleagues, or from other reliable sources at every opportunity. Visit other schools in the borough, seek out friends who are teachers and work elsewhere, use ideas from that very rare INSET day where (for once) the lunch wasn't as memorable as the resources you discovered, or resources that you can download online through social media and websites.

As you evolve throughout your career, you'll get very excited about resources that you've created yourself; you'll be gutted when those resources don't quite hit the mark or take off. Worse still, when students leave behind your carefully, crafted worksheets on the floor – this can be quite soul-destroying!

You can always turn the driest of resources into something inspiring.

MEET & TWEET

Twitter name? @pepsmccrea
Actual name? Peps Mccrea
What's his job? Senior lecturer in teacher education at the University of Brighton, researcher and social entrepreneur
Specialist topic? Innovation in teaching and learning, particularly edtech startups
Why should I follow him? He teaches teachers, writes books and builds great ideas, for example, @staffrm which is a professional learning community for teachers. Check out his website: pepsmccrea.com

MEET & TWEET

Twitter name? @ASTSupportAAli
Actual name? Amjad Ali
What's his job? Secondary assistant headteacher
Specialist topic? Inclusion, teaching and learning
Why should I follow him? He shares hundreds of classroom resources. Check out his website: cheneyagilitytoolkit.blogspot.co.uk

The essential classroom teacher toolkit

PAPERWORK

There are two ways to look at a teacher's desk. If it's tidy, they probably spend too much time at it! If it's messy, full of reports and resources, and you can barely find a keyboard or pen under that pile of marking, then the chances are that this teacher is busy with students.

Here's something you already know: teachers are overburdened with paperwork. Paperwork will haunt you throughout your entire teaching career. In your first year it will be absolute chaos, and you will wonder 'How on earth am I going to get through that pile of work?' By the second year, you may have started to work out what can wait, as well as what needs urgent attention. And by the time you gain more experience, you will have identified the strategies that work best for you and those that do not. This is what you master with experience. After all, not all paperwork in school is linked to the classroom.

Yes, I did say that. Not all paperwork is linked to the main role in your classroom. Sad, isn't it?

As I write this chapter, I consider the reality of my own job during this point of the academic year. We have just passed the Easter season and have entered what colleagues affirm as 'the silly season'. This is when students are entering their final revision period, the mock exams are well and truly over and examination fever is brewing. Pre-public examination preparation is under way and end-of-year reports are building and due for completion.

During the silly season, assessments are also due to be input on to the management information system (your ICT network), so that school reports can be generated numerically, alongside the comments you provide for each child over the preceding six to seven months. This is a huge task. It may be digital, but it's paperwork.

PRIORITISING YOUR PAPERWORK

Consider four levels of paperwork:

1. **Urgent** I need to make sure I do this.
2. **Useful** I may need in the future, so I'll put it somewhere safe.
3. **Useless** I'll throw it into the recycling bin immediately.
4. **Interesting** I'd like to read this, but I don't have any time. I'll put it here for safekeeping.

'Interesting' paperwork is the most difficult. You want to read it and learn something from it, and you know that if you find time to read it, it will contribute to your CPD. However, the choice to read it is on your terms, rather than it being a school policy document that must be read. Therefore finding the time is difficult. I have saved countless paper articles, tucking them into corners of my desk for skimming in the early morning or a cursory glance over lunch. However, the reality is that I look at the documents I keep once every spring clean, or when I am decluttering over the holidays. I find the moment has gone and they head for the recycling bin.

The more you do, the more you will find to do. So, it is essential to know when to stop and to understand what paper is important to keep and what is important to discard. You will need to get your priorities right. Before each term, look at key dates on the calendar and aim to predict pinch points.

Toolkit essential: managing paperwork

1. **Establish a routine and stick to it** Have set times during the school day and at home that you will allocate to paperwork. In fact, I try my hardest not to take any work home, but it would be unfair of me to say that I never do! And I will usually take a huge pile of marking home most (not all) school holidays, with the greatest volume during the Easter holidays when coursework is handed in for assessment.

2. **Use your non-contact time wisely** If you are lucky enough to have non-contact time allocated on your timetable – check your contract, as most schools follow the School teachers' pay and conditions document (STPCD) – use this for its intended purpose: 'preparation, planning and assessment (PPA) time during the school day.' (ATL PPA guidance)

3. **Be organised** Set yourself clear targets to complete specific tasks.

4. **Be systematic** Start by sorting your paperwork, materials and resources, and keeping only the essentials. Find a place for everything to go, as long as it is not out of sight, out of mind! Clean as you go; there is nothing more satisfying than recycling or shredding a piece of paper, but double-check that you don't need it and that it's not confidential. Then, create a system for your paperwork so you know where everything is.

5. **Go paperless** Avoid printing everything off. Read it on a computer screen and save the file. If you don't miss the document, you don't need it!

BEHAVIOUR MANAGEMENT

When it comes to behaviour management in the classroom, there is one key word…

CONSISTENCY

There is no other consideration. Have clear rules and set routines to make sure that what you say sticks, and train students to act on instruction. If you ignore it, you condone it. See through all sanctions you set.

Consistency within any school requires teamwork, quality communication and training, as well as students seeing the consequences of their actions being dealt with fairly, transparently and on an individual needs basis. Consistency is fundamental to what you do as a teacher, whether you are in your first year or your 30th year in the classroom. Once you have got to know your students well, developed very strong and secure relationships, built mutual respect and can secure silence at the drop of a hat, you will naturally find situations where you can start to flex the boundaries of your behaviour management. But at this stage you must be consistent.

WHOLE SCHOOL POLICY

When you do progress to feeling more confident about pushing your behaviour management boundaries, or even now as you decide on adapting rules for your classroom, ensure you are consistent with and never detrimental to whole school policy, or your colleagues who are working day-in, day-out to secure good behaviour across the whole school. According to a TES Professional article, 'maverick teachers ruin behaviour management for everybody else'.

'Every school has a maverick, the teacher that doesn't play by the school's rules and that never looks at the behaviour policy.'

Do not be a maverick. Although, many schools (and students) benefit from having eccentric – dare I say 'nonconformist' – teachers, the eccentric teacher does their colleagues no favours if they are not consistent with the school behaviour policy. You must learn your school behaviour policy as soon as you start at a new school, and whatever your personal touches to behaviour management in the classroom may be, always stick to the whole school policy rules. Whole school behaviour policy rules are there to create consistency across the school, and you must work to uphold this.

In the same article, Paul Dix is quoted as saying:

'You may think this doesn't really impact how you operate in your own classroom, but you would do well to play closer attention. The maverick buys status on the cheap and everyone else pays the price.'

Paul Dix is an expert on behaviour management and he has created 40 tips for NQTs here:

www.pivotaleducation.com/40-tips-for-nqts

My favourites are:

- **Tip 1** Limit the amount of time that you demand the attention of the whole class. Too much Teacher talk promotes low level disruption.

- **Tip 5** Build links with home. Send positive notes home for pupils who are behaving and working well.

- **Tip 30** When bad behaviour strikes, provide 3 clear choices & give pupils time to make a decision

- **Tip 34** Relentlessly pursue children's positive attributes.

- **Tip 39** Land sanctions softly with a reminder of previous good behaviour.

MEET & TWEET

Twitter name? @pivotalpaul

Actual name? Paul Dix

What's his job? Trainer, author and speaker

What is his field of expertise? Behaviour management

Why should I follow him? Great tips on how to deal with the most difficult behaviour in the classroom.

TREAT THEM FAIRLY AND EQUALLY?

It is well known in teaching that being fair and being equal (or being treated equally) are not the same. I always quell any arguments in which students feel aggrieved about not being treated the same by asking them if they would like to be treated individually. In 99% of cases the answer will be a resounding 'yes'. This then gives me the licence as a teacher to give them an appropriate sanction according to their individual needs and the context of the sanction needed.

The secret is to establish with your students the difference between being fair and equal. This will save you a lot of headaches and heartache in the long run. Being equal means treating them the same, but it doesn't mean being treated in the same way. You need to establish this when dealing with bad behaviour.

Being fair means that a teacher must always try to do their best to give every student what they need to be successful. But, what one student and another student need may be very different, and this means things will not always feel equal. This will be the hardest thing for a teacher to establish in the classroom with students. It's a matter of emotion versus sanction.

Toolkit essential: the glower

'The glower' is the innate ability of any experienced teacher to raise one eyebrow, sometimes two, or to frown in a way that causes both eyebrows to adopt all sorts of positions and make the tardiest of students stop in their tracks! I've seen many experienced teachers do it, and seen many a student sit bolt upright to attention as a result. If you notice a colleague doing this, stop and watch – it's fascinating CPD.

My advice: practise at home in the mirror – it will become your secret weapon!

The following is taken from Paul Dix's blog: *'Right you are in detention… er… next Thursday': Delayed sanctions have less impact* (www.pivotaleducation.com/right-you-are-in-detention-er-next-thursday-delayed-sanctions-have-less-impact)

The longer a sanction is delayed, the more disconnected it becomes from the original behaviour. For your higher order sanctions to have the best chance of being effective, they need to be:

- executed as soon as possible (immediately or on the same day)
- not deferred for another adult to impose
- used to reset and reaffirm expectations with the child
- proportionate.

Try to conceive a hierarchy so that you leave the sanctions that are most time-consuming for the students who need your time most, while executing lower level sanctions immediately:

- verbal warning.
- one minute after class (to speak to the teacher about the behaviour and agree what will happen next time).
- moved within the room (away from peers or to sit with the teacher).
- have to help the teacher organise the classroom at break.
- lunch with the teacher.
- impositions (extra work to be completed at home, counter-signed by the parents and brought to you before school the next day).
- reduced after school detention (10 minutes) so that you can supervise them personally.
- early-to-school detention – child reports 10 minutes early to prepare the class alongside the teacher.

BUILD YOUR BEHAVIOUR MANAGEMENT ETHOS

Getting behaviour right is a complex process. You know your students better than me. What works for you might not work for me, and vice versa, so all I can offer you here are the skeletal bones that you can use as a new teacher to build your own behaviour management ethos.

Plan lessons that focus on learning, not the activity Continually impart the success criteria to your students so everyone is clear about the focus of the lesson. This doesn't have to be written down on a whiteboard or in student books; all that needs to happen, is that you and the students know what is.

Be strict when needed, but know when to drop your guard and spend time building bridges and relationships Students will always respect teachers who are firm and fair, and when they clearly know where they stand and where the boundaries lie. They will know what line they can and can't cross, and if they do cross the line, they should understand that they have done so and know when to apologise. Again, consistency is key. Nobody wants someone who is inconsistent and irrational, with mood swings and high dramas. Save the shouting for lunar eclipses!

Quickly stamp out misbehaviour and deal with any student who wishes to disrupt learning as soon as it happens Make it clear that if they choose to break the rules, they will be dealt with immediately. There is no place in my classroom for students to disrupt learning. And when they do – and yes, it does happen, often – they have a firm one-to-one discussion, a warning, then the sanction!

Follow the rules Follow the school behaviour policy, follow your departmental behaviour policy and stick very tightly to your own classroom policy.

Sweat the small stuff You need to do this every day, whatever the context of your school. Behaviour can be unpredictable; it is important thatyou are prepared and have a range of strategies to deploy in every situation and with every type of behaviour. Be prepared to sound like a broken record until behaviour settles down.

What the DfE says

According to the DfE guidance on school discipline and exclusions (www.gov.uk/school-discipline-exclusions/discipline):

'Schools can punish pupils if they behave badly.
Examples of punishments (sometimes called 'sanctions') include:

- a telling-off
- a letter home
- removal from a class or group
- confiscating something inappropriate for school, e.g. mobile phone or MP3 player
- detention.'

THE LOW-DOWN ON DETENTIONS

'Sir, if I don't do this detention, I promise to be well-behaved next lesson, and it means you can go home early to be with your wife and son...'

Detentions – oh the joy! An unavoidable chore... All teachers will need to set a detention at some point, and when this moment arrives, the secret to your success will be understanding **when**, **why** and **how** to set a detention. In addition, and as frustrating as it may sound, you will need the backing of your department and the parents or carers, as well as understanding and cooperation from the student. All this while at the same time managing your demanding workload, trying to follow school procedures and maintaining a good standard of behaviour management.

SETTING DETENTIONS

When it comes to detentions, I've been there, done that and got the T-shirt! I've set every type of detention you can imagine, from setting a detention for one student for all the wrong reasons, to setting detentions for the entire class for all the right reasons (for example, lost equipment – a kitchen knife in a food technology lesson). Some hypocritical, others justified and others because they are just downright needed! I'm afraid to admit that 10 years ago I was setting detentions willy-nilly and giving my students oodles of lines to write. I recently observed this particularly unforgiveable punishment set for a whole class too; it was a depressing sight, especially as half of the class had behaved impeccably throughout the lesson and it was just two or three who had caused mayhem throughout.

So, at the end of a lesson in which students have chatted, distracted each other and generally been messing around, ask yourself this: has every child misbehaved or contributed so badly that you have to keep them all behind after the lesson or for an after-school detention? Every child? Really? And is issuing them with lines really the best way to help them reflect on their behaviour?

A good teacher will maintain good relationships with students, exercise appropriate authority, and act decisively when necessary. When setting any kind of detention, a teacher must keep in mind the need to safeguard students' well-being, in accordance with statutory provisions. This doesn't mean that any detention should be a pleasant experience. No. But it should at least be a productive exercise for you and the student. This simply means setting detentions with a student or group of students – if needed – to maintain high standards of behaviour. Now, I am not saying that setting whole class detentions is justified or not, as there is a different context to every class and every lesson; what you must be sure of, here, is that you are crystal-clear on the reasons for doing so.

DO NOT SET DETENTIONS FOR THE WRONG REASONS

- **As a first step for dealing with your most difficult students** Detentions require some flexibility, as you cannot set one every day. I'm not saying do not set detentions with your most challenging students. Far from it! But what you need to do is be flexible so that you can make a point, rather than rushing straight in and punishing them with a detention. Address the behaviour and ensure that you've communicated to that particular student that there will be a consequence for their poor choices.

- **When you're feeling exhausted, stressed or under the weather** When I am exhausted, stressed or generally angry with my class, I try my best to use emotional intelligence and question whether the detention I'm setting is justified. Not because I'm being soft, but I want to ensure that I am following the school behaviour policy. Am I being fair and rational? Am I overreacting because I have had a bad day or I am getting a head cold?

- **To showboat** Never set detentions to showboat. Whether this is in front of an 'easy class' (generally, well behaved) or a tough class, or especially in front of colleagues because you are concerned about a) what they think, and b) what they see. This is potentially damaging, as it will mar your own logic when setting detentions in the future. Stop the boat now!

DO SET DETENTIONS FOR THE RIGHT REASONS

- **As a deterrent** Set detentions for students who are poorly behaved and disrupting the teaching and learning taking place in the classroom over time.

- **To follow through with consequences you have set** To ensure that what you say as a teacher is actually what you do, and that poor choices do lead to consequences. It is important that the whole class see that you set detentions when a student oversteps the mark. I cannot emphasise this enough, so I'll say it again. It is important that the whole class see that you set detentions when a student oversteps the mark. Humans are social animals and if a child sees a student behaving badly and this is ignored – dare I say, made to seem acceptable in your classroom – then those students observing the poor behaviour will soon mimic it. If you ignore it, you condone it.

- **In line with your school's behaviour policy** Make sure you understand your school's behaviour policy and set detentions accordingly. In schools where I have worked, and where I've seen behaviour policies work well, everyone understands the system. In these cases, they are simple and clear, and you'll often find students correcting teachers – particularly those having a bad day or who are consistently below par – when they do not follow the whole school system. If this happens, the policy works.

MANAGING DETENTIONS

Following through with detentions involves a bit of effort on your part. Firstly because it consumes your energy beyond the time already allocated to you for your marking, planning and teaching. The last thing teachers need is extra, unwanted time with students who have been misbehaving. However, you will need to invest time in detentions to ensure that behaviour in your class is at the highest standard it can possibly be, and in line with school expectations. Plus, it is worth it in the long run, even though at times you will be sick and tired of repeating the same messages and sanctions over and over again to your students. You'll often feel like a parrot! But, as I've said before, it will be unavoidable for you to opt out of setting detentions, and it is something that you will need to do (a lot) in the earlier years of your career until you establish yourself as a solid classroom practitioner.

Ask yourself the following:

1. Has the student overstepped the line?

2. Have they already been given their last chance/final warning?

3. If you do not set a detention, are you undermining the school behaviour policy?

4. Is the detention focused on the primary behaviour – i.e. the original misdemeanour?

5. When is the best time to complete the detention for you/the student?

DID YOU KNOW?

According to government legislation, as cited in the DfE school discipline and exclusions guidance: 'Schools don't have to give parents notice of after-school detentions or tell them why a detention has been given.' Of course, many schools would want to avoid this, and promote a clear and supportive behaviour policy to enable all students to learn. Student planners and a school's code of conduct may help communicate a school's expectations to parents and students.

RESILIENCE TIP

If you can crack the behaviour in your classroom, you will find that you need to set fewer and fewer detentions. This will be a good indication that you are becoming more and more resilient, but never, ever stop setting detentions as a badge of honour or a way of freeing up your time. It will only lead to further complications in your classroom…

When setting one-to-one and group detentions, always safeguard yourself by considering the following:

1. Does this student have any particular needs you should be aware of? For example, will their parents be aggrieved if you are alone with them in the classroom? I have had some students say: 'My dad will beat me up if they see that I am home later than expected.' What would you do?

2. Does the student know about the detention?

3. Does the student's family know about the detention? If notice is required, has there been a telephone call, a text alert or a letter home?

4. If necessary, has the relevant staff member been informed?

5. Where will the detention be?

6. Will you and the student be in clear sight of others? If this is a vulnerable student, how could you organise the sanction to suit both parties?

7. How long is the detention, and what you are you expecting the student to do during the time?

8. What will you do? Have you worked out exactly what you need to say to the student? How will you do this? Will it be within earshot of other students or teachers?

9. What will be the follow-up, and when? In the next lesson? With colleagues and parents?

10. And finally, have you used the opportunity to rebuild any relationship to ensure that teaching and learning can continue? This is vital to reduce the chance of the event being repeated.

WHAT WOULD YOU DO?

Tweet me @TeacherToolkit

PARENTS & CARERS

In your role as a teacher, you will need to communicate effectively with parents and carers with regard to students' achievements, behaviour and well-being. Address both positive and negative issues. You will need to do this with clarity, consistency, composure and resilience. Parents' evenings are obvious times for this to happen, and these are discussed on page 148. In this chapter, the focus is on the communication that happens the rest of the time.

You cannot speak with every single parent or carer in your day-to-day teaching throughout the academic year, but you can have a damn good crack at it. And, although teaching is all-consuming, working with parents is often one of those unexpectedly rewarding aspects of the job.

POSITIVE FEEDBACK AND GOOD NEWS

There is nothing more simple and powerful than a positive phone call in the evening to whoever is at home. Do not underestimate the importance of this type of humble communication. It takes 30 seconds to do, and it's what builds positive relationships from the classroom to home. You will also feel better, too!

WHAT TO PRAISE?

- **Achievement** Let parents know when their child has won awards or made other achievements at school. Bypass all the official mechanisms such as online award platforms, stickers and comments to students in class. A phone call home works wonders. Failing that, if the students in your school use a planner, a simple sentence that parents can read will suffice.

- **Well-being** Parents and carers love to know that their children are happy at school. Who wouldn't? Whatever situation you find yourself in, whether it's a parents' evening or a phone call in the evening, remember to say: 'Hi. Your son/daughter is working very well in class and appears to be very healthy and happy at school. I just wanted to let you know.'

- **Positive contributions** If you see a child making a positive contribution in school and outside of your classroom, make sure you tell them. This may be picking up a piece of litter, welcoming a visitor to the school, holding a door open for a teacher carrying a heavy load of books, or playing a leading role in the school performance. Quash any myths you have heard about them being shy in class! Whatever it is, make sure you congratulate them and say thank you by communicating with parents and carers at home. It's often these small conversations and moments of praise and reassurance that make the biggest impact on a child's life.

COMMUNICATING STUDENTS' LEARNING

In your first year of teaching, working with parents and carers will become quite a familiar experience. After all, you are dealing with their children! But during that year, your main focus will naturally be to deal with marking, lesson planning, and teaching. As you get to grips with these three basic core components, two of these will directly link with parents, and the other will have an indirect link.

- **Marking** A direct link is communicating with parents via marking. Mark your students' books with due care and attention, and do it well. Where possible, do it regularly (while still managing your workload and work–life balance carefully) to ensure that parents are aware of what is being assessed when they look through their child's books.

- **Planning** The indirect link is your lesson planning. Under-plan or over-plan, pitch too high or too low and you may find an unexpected phone call from home. I know I have. Remember that you and your lessons get summed up in a single word – or at best a sentence – by your students to someone inquisitive at home. Bang! There's your teacher reputation shared in a snapshot with the family. It may be star-studded, or you may be sold down the river by an 11-year-old. So, plan well or expect parents to find out!

- **Teaching** If possible, create a system where students take books home and safely return them with people at home involved in the process. What goes on in schools is always a four-way deal: the teacher, the child, the parents/carers, the school. Providing regular comments in your books and encouraging students to take them home can become a very sophisticated way of involving parents/carers in their child's education.

Toolkit essential: managing homework with parents and carers

Other aspects of homework are addressed in the chapter on Homework, page 63.

1. **Not all parents have time to help** Set tasks that students can complete themselves.

2. **Use your school website or social media to log homework set** If parents or carers can access the details, then there can be no confusion as to what the task is, what is required and when. Consider online language translations.

3. **Don't assume parents/carers have subject knowledge** Many parents may have left education – and learning – at least 10 to 20 years ago. If I were helping my son in ten years' time with homework on photosynthesis, I may remember the basic principles, but ask me for details and I would have to go back to the drawing board and revise.

4. **Set specific homework tasks to involve the family** It is great to set an engaging piece of homework to involve family at home from time to time, but make sure you do not penalise students who are unable to do so, for obvious reasons. Make it an option to work alongside someone else.

MAKE THAT CALL

There are many ways of communicating with parents, but I want to focus on the phone call. You may think it trite to write about something as simple as a phone call, but do not underestimate the influence this can have.

Toolkit essential: making phone calls

1. **Stand up!** I once read that standing up while on the phone increases immediacy. Try it. I feel sharper on my feet, pacing back and forth. It's quite a subliminal way to ensure your conversation is straight to the point, whether the reason for it is positive or negative behaviour.

2. **Prepare a script in advance** This can help you keep a phone call concise.

3. **Use a crib sheet** See opposite. It makes sure you don't miss anything out.

4. **Thank them** Always thank the parent/carer for their support.

5. **School ethos** Always ensure that you are re-emphasising the school ethos and the school behaviour policy.

6. **Keep to the point** Ensure that you have all the facts and that you focus on the primary behaviour and the consequence. Do not go into details and start making it a tit-for-tat conversation. The phone call will lose impact.

7. **Have the student in the room** Place the parent on loudspeaker and have the student listen to the call. It's fascinating to see and hear how students respond. This has a high impact!

8. **Positive phone calls on a Friday evening** This is a great end to a tiring week on your part, but also gives you the opportunity to share some good news with families for the weekend. It also makes sure you go home with a spring in your step.

9. **Sleep on it** Particularly with emotive issues, it is often better to wait 24 hours before contacting home.

10. **Phoning before school** I've made positive phone calls home at 7am. I've even made negative phone calls then too. Always consider the impact this may have at home on the child and the family. It is a busy time – they are all getting ready for work and school. I do not represent every human being, but what would make anyone want to pick up a phone at 7am, only for the teacher to give them some negative news? It would certainly put me in a grumpy mood. What effect would this then have on the child later on that day when you see them in class? I've been there and done it – it can work both ways.

Phone call crib sheet

1. I'm just calling to update you on (student's) progress.
2. Is it a good time to talk?
3. Share the specific detail/action/outcome.
4. Thank you for your support.
5. Any questions? Have a lovely evening/day.

DEALING WITH HARD TO REACH PARENTS/CARERS

The vast majority of parents will want to know how their child is doing at school. Your school has an obligation to communicate with home on a number of occasions per academic year, and as a teacher it is your job to perform this duty and be directly involved in working with parents, especially as a form tutor (see page 79). Several times a year you will be asked to complete reports about the students that you teach. In some circumstances, parental engagement, or lack of it, may be a warning that things at home are not as good as they could be for certain students.

Do you think that the parents or carers do not care? If that student does not have an immediate family member at home, will someone else show any concern – whether positive or negative – about the school news of this child?

Some parents just do not want to know anything about their child in school. Having worked in challenging schools in some of the most deprived boroughs in London, I sadly have worked with countless students with hard to reach families. There are a million and one reasons for this, but the evidence is clear – home support does have an impact on student outcomes in the classroom.

CONSULT YOUR COLLEAGUES

I cannot recommend strongly enough that all new teachers should consult experienced colleagues within their school when it comes to working with hard to reach parents and carers. There will be people designated as safeguarding lead, child protection officers, counsellors and psychologists, education welfare officers, those who travel with the school bus and so forth.

I have often narrowly avoided making several mistakes, were it not for the support of established colleagues who were able to share key information before I made any contact home. Hard to reach parents are hard to reach for a reason. Do your research. Speak with your head of year or a child's form tutor and establish relationships with colleagues who have worked in the school for many years, and get as much information as possible before making contact home. Never make a call home without having researched the basic information on that child and their family. Your colleagues will have plenty of knowledge regarding individual students and home circumstances to share with you. This can often explain unusual circumstances in the classroom, behaviour and even what is written in exercise books!

SCHOOL DUTIES

Some quick calculations:

Per week:	1 x 20 minutes break duty	= 20 minutes
Per year:	38 weeks per academic year	= 38 x 20 minutes
		= 12 hours 40 minutes per year

Consider my 17 years of teaching...

This crudely equates to an equivalent of 215 hours and 20 minutes.

Without doubt you will have to complete a break or lunchtime duty in the course of your career. Your school may or may not provide supervisors to do this, but either way, the likelihood of you standing in on a duty of some kind to support the safety of the children out of lessons is a given.

OBLIGATIONS AND CONSIDERATIONS

Duties will cover a range of obligations, from the unremarkable break duty to having to stand in the cold rain at the school gate on a drab, dreary and cold Thursday morning in February! So, why write about this, you ask? Well, there are up sides and down sides to being given a duty of some kind, and this experience can make or break you. However, no school I know offers CPD for being on break duty!

BREAK DUTY PROS

1. You get some fresh air (not really a positive if you are a PE teacher).

2. You see students in a different context.

3. You get to speak with students outside of the classroom.

4. You can meet and chat with colleagues you would not normally see day-to-day.

5. You are a visual presence, which is a small, yet important, contribution to upholding behaviour levels in the school. It's no secret that students will not be up to any tricks if they can see a teacher.

BREAK DUTY CONS

1. It's the last thing you want to do when you are already feeling exhausted.

2. No, it really is the last thing you want to do when you have a lesson straight after your duty, or you've got other things to be doing, such as reports or marking.

3. It's often freezing or wet!

4. You risk losing your mug of coffee as a student runs past you on the corridor.

5. You know there is a high chance you will see a kerfuffle, and that you will have to deal with it. This will also require paperwork.

BEST PRACTICE

In the best examples I can think of, teachers get creative! Perhaps this means offering to host a 15-minute ICT session, which will allow students to complete or print off their homework, or take part in a school project and work on their own literacy by completing online reading tests. You name it; anything is possible. Offering to run a society or duty could take 20–30 students off the playground or out of the corridors and into a classroom for more structured activities (but not necessarily additional curriculum time).

Get to know students you may have difficulties with in class, and engage with them in the playground. This is their territory. I witnessed one teacher who played basketball with the most challenging students in our school every single break duty. This was not only great exercise for him and them, but when it mattered back in the classroom or on the corridors, they were putty in his hands. Why? Because he had been on their level, building a relationship with them outside of his teaching subject. Win-win!

BE PREPARED

So let's assume, whether you like the fresh air and interacting with students or not, completing a duty of sorts is not something you will prioritise – particularly a wet and windy break duty on a Tuesday morning (which often tends to be the time when students get a little lively). It helps to be prepared.

Toolkit essential: surviving school duties

- Arrive early and leave late (where possible).

- Keep your wits about you. Your hardiness will be tested at the best of times: wind; rain; snow; incidents of bullying; scuffles and banter.

- Have a back-up plan. If you do your duty with a colleague, plan for when things need to change due to an illness, an observation… or the time you forget!

- Locate your nearest support (for example, a more experienced colleague) in case of emergency.

- Locate your nearest fire alarm and fire exit.

- Who is your nearest first-aider?

- Locate the nearest telephone (and not your mobile phone).

- Locate the nearest toilet, should you need to go.

- Have a whistle and make sure you know the school rules, especially the rules for being outside.

- Some schools provide high-visibility jackets. If they are not provided, suggest it or make sure you are walking around and being seen and heard.

In my experience, you will either make friends with a new colleague (outside of your department) and design a biscuit rota together, or it can be a lonely and depressing experience. It shouldn't be that way. Rarely do schools or leaders offer anyone support in schools when on duty though. Support? 'What support do you need to be able to stand "your patch" on the playground?' I once was told…

WHAT NOT TO DO

I'm sure we can all rattle off a long list of pet hates; well, these are mine. Don't commit these school duty atrocities:

- Do not turn up late to find a member of the senior leadership team standing in your place, frowning and tapping the cold concrete floor with the tip of their shoes.
- Do not stand in a corner of the playground, talking to colleagues and ignoring the students.
- Do not leave early, very early…
- Do not use a mobile phone (against school policy) in front of the entire school.
- Do not forget to organise cover when you know in advance you will be absent.
- Do not ignore a volatile situation.
- Do not ignore bad language, spitting or litter being dropped on the floor.
- Do not just stand there. No presence. No interaction with students. No communication.

SCHOOL DUTIES HERO!

Embrace break time. Gain a reputation for being the member of staff who runs around all the duty locations saying hello to everyone and handing out chocolates, hard-boiled sweeties or cups of tea. Even hassle a member of the leadership team for a small budget to fund a box of chocolates per week. Call it staff well-being!

RESILIENCE TIP

The more duties that you do, the more experience you gain. Over the course of one academic year, there is a high chance you will see, hear and touch a range of events, moods and stories. Be prepared for the unexpected and keep your wits about you. Oh, and it's not daft to ask for training. It can be easily fixed by you shadowing a senior member of staff and asking them to point out what they see as you walk around the school together. I'm certain it will prove insightful and help you develop a little resilience and hardiness in all aspects of school life.

PROFESSIONAL CONDUCT

'Teachers uphold public trust in the profession and maintain high standards of ethics and behaviour, within and outside school.'
(DfE, Teachers' Standards)

This includes Friday night at the pub, on social media and driving in your car! In many school communities, you might know every single person. The students you teach may be the children of your best friends. What happens when you need to tell them off? At what point do you stop becoming a teacher with a student you teach if you interact with their family out of school hours? It's a tricky one.

TOEING THE LINE

Ask yourself how many of the following statements or questions you have found yourself thinking, overhearing or saying in class:

1. Right, you answer those questions while I just nip out for a fag.*

2. Here is my personal email address.*

3. During this term, I'm not going to mark any of your books.

4. OK. Hands up – who doesn't understand?

5. Don't choose that subject at GCSE, it won't help you (insert)…

6. Why didn't you do your homework? It was easy.

7. If you need help, ask your mum to text me.*

8. You only need to learn this for the exam, then you can forget it.

9. I haven't planned anything today and I've forgotten what I'm doing. Can you lot just get on with some colouring in or just read a book…

10. My other class did this really well. What's wrong with you today?

11. You have to be here, I don't.

12. Who's your teacher? (Reply) Well, that explains it. They're not even a proper teacher…*

13. 'Hello mum? Sorry, I'm teaching. I can't speak right now.'

14. Stand in the corner and put your hands on your head.*

15. God. I was hammered at the weekend!*

Much of the above is written in jest – but jest with caution; you are the professional.
* The statements highlighted with a small asterisk should be avoided at all costs. (These are all safeguarding and/or health and safety issues.)

CODE OF CONDUCT

We all need a benchmark. A code of conduct ensures we all work within a clear set of professional standards. Here is an example:

- To 'have proper and professional regard for the ethos, policies and practices of the school in which they teach' (DfE Teachers' Standards), while maintaining good standards of teaching. That is every teacher's **raison d'être**.

- To 'have an understanding of, and always act within, the statutory frameworks which set out their professional duties and responsibilities' (DfE Teachers' Standards) apart from what they may or may not do in their personal life, is essential.

- Every teacher must 'show tolerance of and respect for the rights of others'. (DfE Teachers' Standards) This is not just colleagues, but students and visitors to the school as well.

There has been an increasing amount of media attention given to the importance of British values in schools today, including: democracy, the rule of law, individual liberty and respect. Following Peter Clarke's report covering the findings of his investigation into Birmingham schools and the 'Trojan Horse' incident, we are reminded that we should be tolerant of those with different faiths and beliefs, regardless of which school we work in – even if it is a faith school – and that we must 'challenge extremist views'.

As teachers, we must always be mindful not to promote our own personal views to children, ensuring that personal beliefs are not expressed in ways that exploit students' vulnerability or might lead them to break the law.

What the DfE says

As a new teacher, you will need to learn very quickly how to treat with dignity the students and wide variety of colleagues you will work with, building relationships at all times and observing proper boundaries appropriate to a teacher's professional position. You will need to have regard for the need to safeguard students' well-being, in accordance with statutory provisions. The DfE document *Keeping children safe in education* is essential reading for every teacher, and helps us to understand the nature of our responsibilities beyond our classroom. It is compulsory for all teachers to read at least Part 1 of this document. (www.gov.uk/government/publications/keeping-children-safe-in-education--2) When did you last read it?

PUTTING IT INTO PRACTICE

Without teaching you how to suck eggs, my advice is to ensure that you maintain your professional conduct, no matter what experiences come your way. Consider these reflection questions:

1. How is this profession different from any other kind of job?

2. Do your professional judgements reveal particular values?

3. What impact or influence must you have on children in your care?

I am certain the answers to some of the above questions will be fascinating, and everyone will have different answers. Withholding a level of decorum in and out of school comes with the territory, I'm afraid. Of course, I'm not saying you can't go to the pub on a Friday night, or post your status on social media, but as you become more experienced in teaching, professionalism will come more and more naturally to you. In your personal and professional life you must withhold a certain level of conduct. Uphold public trust in the profession and maintain high standards of ethics and behaviour, both within and outside of school.

Dress smart.

Think twice.

Be on time.

Also, don't steal from the workplace, even if it's a ream of paper from the reprographics room. After all, it's school property, not for your printer at home!

Striking is never an easy decision to make as a teacher, and should always be the last resort. ⟶

INDUSTRIAL ACTION

At some point in your career, the potential for taking strike action will arise. Throughout my career I have taken strike action, but I've also been in a position where I was unable to strike for various reasons. For example, to attend an interview, even though half of the staff of the school I was visiting were also off-site!

Whatever your views on strike action, it must be made clear to you that if you are part of the union you will be obligated to strike. But this does not mean that you have to do it! For whatever reason – this could be particular circumstances or your own personal views – you could decide not to. Whatever the circumstances, make sure you know all the facts, do your reading, talk to colleagues and speak to your headteacher if necessary before making your decision.

YOUR WELL-BEING

'...over half of teachers (52%) say that they have seriously considered leaving their current job in the last 12 months and nearly half (47%) have seriously considered leaving the profession.'

This eye-watering statistic is from the NASUWT teachers' satisfaction and well-being in the workplace survey, conducted by ComRes. You can read more shocking statistics in this report at the link below, including that 'Teachers' biggest concern regarding their job is workload (79%)'.

Note, the research was conducted by polling agency ComRes, who interviewed 501 teachers in England between the 30th October and 10th November 2013.

Another interesting report is the *Workload challenge: analysis of teacher responses*, published by the DfE. This report uncovered that 'two specific tasks… were reported as being burdensome for the majority of sample respondents: recording, inputting, monitoring and analysing data (56%) and excessive/depth of marking detail and frequency required (53%).'

NASUWT teachers' satisfaction and well-being in the workplace survey: www.comres.co.uk/polls/nasuwt-teachers-satisfaction-and-wellbeing-in-the-workplace-survey

Workload challenge: www.gov.uk/government/publications/workload-challenge-analysis-of-teacher-responses

FIVE-POINT PLAN FOR SENIOR LEADERS AND SCHOOL MANAGEMENT TEAM

Follow this five-point plan to improve teacher well-being in your school.

1. **Accountability** Keep expectations high, but remain flexible. Remove unnecessary checklists and allow teachers to teach in a style that suits the students in their classroom. For example: remove the burden of lesson planning and marking by banishing lesson proformas from appraisal observations and day-to-day teaching and learning; ensure all staff are clear about the expectations of marking – that every page in a student's book does not have to be marked (see page 7); streamline reporting, assessment, flexible timetable and working arrangements.

2. **Workload** Reduce unnecessary workload on staff – endless meetings, tick-box proformas and mocksteds! (See page 47.) Don't have meetings for meetings' sake. If you do have a meeting, publish agendas and handouts in advance. Hold shorter 30-minute meetings to bring staff together for clarification or a Q&A session, and limit attendance to meetings to only include staff concerned. Trust staff to do the job, and if they can't meet expectations, adapt and refine what is expected and have 'that conversation', but be flexible.

3. **Professional development** The school CPD budget should be huge: at least 1–2% of the overall school budget! Invest in your staff by providing tailored, differentiated in-house CPD for every adult within the school.

4. **Attrition** Eradicate bullies, taskmasters and leaders who berate adults within the school who are overwhelmed with remedial tasks and heavy-handed, ill-thought-out workload. Insist that the government, unions and policymakers reduce the need for rapid change and start to consolidate the changes that have been made since 2010. What works best is good teaching and learning in the classroom. Everything else is peripheral. Teaching will always be a noble profession, but certainly not one that has credibility if we do not retain and invest in staff.

5. **Genuine support** A meaningful and realistic vision for staff well-being is needed for every school. Happy schools have happy teachers, and happy and healthy teachers make happy schools and achieve happy outcomes. But in order to achieve this, every member of staff, no matter how jaded, needs support and guidance. Staff need to be listened to carefully. In everyone, there is a real potential. As school leaders, managers or appraisers, we need to find this potential and unlock it. Give every member of staff a linked coach/mentor as well as an appraiser and the time to work on this aspect. The coach/mentor can actually meet to support staff well-being and personal and professional CPD needs in a structured/calendared way.

THREE-POINT PLAN FOR TEACHERS

You need to look after yourself; being a teacher is a very, very stressful profession.

Here is a very simple three-point plan:

1. Sleep. **2.** Eat well. **3.** Switch off.

Having said that, I'm writing this chapter after an 11-hour day in school. And, the funny thing is that as I'm writing this book I'm talking more and more about education and not switching off! Secretly – despite the long hours, the pressures, the negativity, the feeling of being unappreciated, the many difficulties, the seemingly constant media coverage of our jobs, and so on – most of us do love it and there is nothing we would rather do. We just need to remember that when it's hard-going!

A recent BBC article based on an international OCED study reported:

> *'Despite this sense of being unappreciated, there were still high levels of job satisfaction - with a large majority saying they would choose teaching again as a career choice.' This is even though 'teachers in England are working 46 hours per week in term time, considerably above the international average of 38 hours.'*

It is very important during your entire career that you have a specific time and place where you can be away from the computer, away from the work environment and sometimes even away from home to do things for yourself. I know this will not always be possible for everyone, because all of us have our own commitments out of school hours, such as childcare and family. Here are some of the things I have done:

• been a semi-professional footballer

• written a book!

Obviously, during the holidays you have much more time to yourself. And you might find yourself highly likely to be jetting abroad overseas and, depending on your circumstances, this type of activity will change over the course of your career. For example, in my earlier years I once went abroad 11 times in one year whereas now, with my son in my life, I've not been abroad for over four years!

RESILIENCE TIP

Teaching is a lifetime's craft. You will never perfect it, nor complete your to do list. Accept this early on and you will already begin to master the art of resilience: know when to stop, when to switch off and when it is time to look after you!

#INTELLIGENT

2

INTELLIGENT

'It was all laid out ready to go for the best demonstration any trainee teacher could prepare for. Do you think it went according to plan?'

BE INTELLIGENT

My second year of teaching was probably one of the most enjoyable of my career and hopefully you'll enjoy yours just as much. You have your first year under your belt and, unless you're moving schools, you already know the staff, students and school systems much better than before. You are now in a position to start to take more time to really think about your teaching.

The second section of this book is not just about your second year in teaching; it's about becoming, being and remaining an 'intelligent' teacher. This is the second part that makes up the whole Vitruvian teacher, and it refers to using your intelligence as a teacher in a variety of areas; developing the problem-solving skills, knowledge and experience needed to yield successful outcomes in all students; taking a moment to think about your precious time and how to use it wisely; starting to develop your own self- and peer-reflection skills and developing your emotional intelligence.

WHY INTELLIGENCE?

In your first year of teaching, you will grow in confidence and secure a firmer grip of the basics, especially the mark, plan, teach, repeat model (hopefully). However, you probably won't yet have mastered the process of 'thinking about teaching', and year two is when you need to start working towards becoming a thoughtful teacher. For instance, you may know how to use a lesson plan to plot out what you are going to teach today, tomorrow and next week, but you may not yet have really thought about every single child in your class and how you will get the best out of each individual. You may not yet have started to really reflect on the best ways to assess and track your students' progress, and you probably have not yet thought about how observations can actually be a good thing.

Being 'intelligent' doesn't necessarily mean having lots of knowledge. It's about understanding what has an impact on students, and what can be discarded as

unnecessary effort. For example, lengthy lesson plans, focusing on the activity and not the learning can go, in favour of having more useful thoughts about teacher pedagogy, including using data, differentiating and carefully planning homework.

I start this section with some tips on time management. Start by thinking intelligently about the time you have. If you can use fleeting moments of available time to think and plan ahead, to make informed decisions, to use time more wisely to help students in your class to make progress, then you may be on your way to great teaching.

Becoming a fully functional teacher is something that takes many years to master, but in your second year you have every chance of building on and securing the good foundations that should set you up for a long and happy career. Every teacher should be able to self-evaluate their own practice and receive feedback from colleagues. As your career develops, you will be expected to widen your subject knowledge, skill and understanding to match the context of where you are working. In everything you do, you must take what you know about teaching thus far, and extend the breadth of your expertise so that you can continue to set high expectations, promote good progress, demonstrate good subject knowledge, plan and teach well, adapt to the needs of all students, make accurate use of assessment and feedback, as well as manage behaviour effectively. It's a long list, but if you can achieve this, you will be taking full responsibility for improving your own teaching through self-reflection and analysis of your own practice. This is vital – it is learning to be 'intelligent'.

If you can develop a degree of awareness, the likelihood is, that as you establish your own pedagogy, you will be invited to start using your experience with others; more on this in the Collaborative section of this book (section 4).

From section 1, we have learnt that in your first year of teaching, a resilient interior and exterior is needed until you are established. This does not mean that you cannot smile before Christmas(!),

nor does it mean that you reduce the emotional connections with your students. Being resilient just means growing a tough shell to be able to deal with the influx of information, emotion and sensations that will come your way.

In this section, you can expect to be exposed to a wide range of thoughtful issues in education that – over time – you will need to evolve a deep knowledge and understanding of. This will ensure that you can develop your teaching in an 'intelligent way' once you have a) toughened up and b) developed a thoughtful insight into what, why and how you do the things you do, as well as the external factors that will invade your classroom space. You will need to make good use of assessment and track progress to help your students improve, and you will need to support pupil premium students and develop strategies for differentiation as well as the emotional armoury to support over 25 students in a tutor group. All in all, you need to develop a little more intelligence – and by this I mean an awareness – in order to survive and develop Vitruvian teaching.

TIME MANAGEMENT

You've completed your first year and you have the basics sorted. It's now your second year of teaching and your timetable has increased. You need to think intelligently about how to manage your time – how to get organised and start working smarter.

As you would expect of a chapter on time management, I intend to keep this short and to the point. However, I am so passionate about this issue – about how to cut all the nonsense out of teaching and streamline it – that I do go on a little bit, so please bear with me. It will be worth it!

We are all pushed for time, but it's no excuse. The demands placed on educators in **any** type of classroom, coupled with the expectation for planning to meet the needs of all students, and the expectations placed on teacher's systems and management create unnecessary bureaucracy.

It doesn't matter what your role or responsibility is in school, managing and effectively using your time will always have a significant effect on what you can achieve in your work. For teachers new to the profession, developing the art of time management will be a steep learning curve. You will need to come to terms with deadlines, the highs and lows of workload throughout the academic term, requests made by colleagues in your department (and outside your department, for example, as a form tutor) and then of course the demands placed on you by students and parents. Most of this should be expected, but inevitably there will be the unexpected.

With unexpected events and demands, it is vital that you have secure time management strategies in place to deal with additional stresses placed upon you. For the vast majority of teachers, the contact ratio is between 0.75 and 0.9 for most full-time equivalent teachers. Although the strain placed on teachers and the timetable is common practice and almost taken for granted, we should never accept it, nor allow it to be become a burden.

Toolkit essential: time-saving techniques

(These are described in more detail in other chapters of this book, as indicated.)

- Give direct instruction, which is highly engaging for students (see Homework, page 63).

- Simplify lesson planning and improve marking so that students act on feedback (see, Paperwork, page 20 and Assessment, Feedback & Progress, page 49).

- Design assessments that require student responsibility (see Inspiring Lessons, page 92).

- Set inspiring, differentiated and self-selecting homework (see Homework, page 63).

- Identify ways to gather evidence in observations of self/peers (see Observations, page 68).

- Review teaching and shift pedagogy to be a leader of learning (see Middle Leadership, page 174).

TIME-SAVING TO DO LIST

☑ Keep in the know

My key piece of advice would be this: know your objectives; know your deadlines; know the importance of each task – because somebody else will be relying on you to complete something, even if it is just to put pen to paper.

☑ Prioritise

Having identified a time management issue, it is worth pausing for a moment to consider a) whether it is important and b) its potential impact. A simple question to ask yourself is: 'What would happen if I didn't complete this task at this moment in time?' Not everything can be important and some things don't have a particularly high impact. Why not categorise tasks as medium (M) or low (L) priority. Consider the importance and potential impact of tasks on the quality of your teaching, or the care, support or guidance of children. It is vital that you determine your priorities daily, weekly and termly.

☑ Abandon

We seem to be far better at increasing our workload than decreasing it. It's important to create the time and space to do a smaller number of tasks very well. There may be whole sets of activities or individual tasks that can be binned and consigned to history. Some may never have been that important nor have had any real impact. Every time you add something to your own or another person's workload, you should commit to also taking something away. However, there is a high chance that as a new teacher it will not be you assigning tasks for others, but others assigning tasks for you. Be bold and brave! Ask your line manager what you should abandon in order to meet this deadline, or at least if it's not possible, make them aware of the current pressures you may be under.

☑ Do more, do less

In order to improve your time management intelligence, and a slightly less drastic step than abandonment, doing more or doing less requires careful analysis of the various tasks you are required to complete. What would you do more or less of when planning for your classes, or tracking progress, or ensuring high-quality feedback for students?

☑ Increase capacity

One important way to improve your effectiveness and decrease time wasted is to increase your individual capacity. Complete administrative tasks in meetings; consider effective use of technology to manage information better, for example, using Google Docs to collaborate.

INTELLIGENCE TIP

A heavy workload, minimal non-contact time and having to factor in unplanned events such as additional deadlines will take their toll on you. Take control of your time sooner rather than later, because if you don't, either the work will take control of you, or someone else will give you even more things to do.

ASSESSMENT, FEEDBACK & PROGRESS

Teacher or student, we all grow as learners by receiving feedback.

'Great teaching equates to prior learning which is assessed systematically and accurately.'

As discussed at length in section 1, marking a class set of books and using the evidence to inform your planning and teaching is the most important skill for you learn in your first year of teaching. Once you have got a handle on the teaching, you need to start thinking more intelligently about how you are marking, what methods you are using and how you are generally using and planning assessment in your classroom to measure and ensure progress.

BEING INTELLIGENT

As teachers, we must:

- have a secure overview of the starting points, progress and context of all students;
- make accurate and productive use of assessment;
- know and understand how to assess relevant subject and curriculum areas, as well as statutory assessment requirements when submitting students' work for public examination;
- make use of formative and summative assessment to secure students' progress, even though every piece of work need not be assessed;
- ensure that marking, assessment and feedback happens regularly;
- use relevant data to monitor progress, set targets, and plan subsequent lessons (see the chapter that follows for more on data (page 55);
- have a clear understanding of the needs of all students in any class, including those with additional learning needs and those exceeding expectations, and be able to use and evaluate distinctive teaching approaches to engage and support them.

Assessment will always inform your planning; it is instant differentiation and is the most powerful thing you can do as a teacher.

I have to confess that this has been the hardest chapter of this book for me to write. Why? you might ask.

THE PROBLEMS WITH ASSESSMENT

- Firstly, the national landscape of assessment is changing and the profession is currently (as I write) left with no national framework for assessing student work throughout Key Stages 1–3.

- Secondly, although I admit that as teachers we cannot live without assessment, as an individual, assessment just sends shivers down my spine. It reminds me of the endless pile of marking that needs to be completed before an assessment is apportioned to a piece of work.

But why am I out of love with assessment?

In section 1 I highlighted the importance of marking students' work, and giving clear feedback so that they can act upon it. Mark less, but give students regular feedback – both orally and through accurate assessment – and encourage students to respond to the feedback depending on their needs.

However, recent conversations with English teachers have shown me just how difficult this all is. The workload and expectations in that subject, for example, are relentless. The depth and detail that is expected of their marking, for example by examination boards for a high number of controlled assessments, is overwhelming. No matter what the marking policy in your school says to help address teacher workload, these external expectations, as well as our own desire to assess well for the sake of our students, makes it all very difficult to achieve.

So, the big issue is: how can marking and assessment be appropriately and sensitively streamlined to help reduce workload?

> 'MARKING SHOULD BE A PRIORITY, AND I AM STILL FAILING TO MAKE IT MY NUMBER ONE PRIORITY AFTER 20 YEARS! I WONDER IF MARKING IS A POISONED CHALICE? THAT NO MATTER WHAT WE DO OR SAY, IT WILL ALWAYS BE A BURDEN; LIKE A NIGGLING PAIN IN YOUR SIDE THAT JUST WON'T GO AWAY. AS SOON AS IT'S FIXED IT COMES BACK A WEEK LATER...'
>
> @TeacherToolkit

If we are all to improve our vision for marking and assessment, it must always be tackled from a full-time classroom teacher's perspective. Take a look at the full-time classroom teacher's profile.

PROFILE: full-time secondary classroom teacher*

- **Teaches** 20 periods per week (1-hour lessons from a 25-hour timetable)
- **Timetable** 25 hours (leaving 5 hours of non-contact time)
- **Classes** 15 different classes (non-core subject such as drama with one period per KS3 class)
- **Marking** A possible 450 books (based on 30 students per class)
- **Per 7-week term** 3,150 possible book interactions and marking opportunities!

*Figures are estimated.

Yes! That's over 3,000 possible opportunities to assess and mark work! How can we expect this teacher to complete all the work in the allocated time, considering that some after-school time is dedicated to meetings, enrichment and extra-curricular clubs? It is totally unrealistic to expect to be able to do this, never mind do it well.

So, how can you approach assessment in order to ensure that you maintain a sensible work–life balance and a decent level of well-being, while also ensuring student books are marked so that students can progress?

Whatever you end up doing in your school, make sure it works for you and your students; of course this must be in-line with your whole-school marking policy to ensuring that what you do has any impact. And for goodness sake, please make sure you are marking for your students and not the Grim Reaper!

Five-point plan for assessment

This is what we should all aim for:

1. To develop high-quality assessment.
2. To develop diagnostic feedback across all subjects.
3. To approach marking from a realistic workload perspective.
4. To keep in mind a common-sense approach.
5. To ensure we are getting it right for students and teachers from the outset.

PUTTING IT INTO PRACTICE

Toolkit essential: managing assessment workload

1. Attach work to displays around the classroom with banners indicating success criteria.

2. Share the success criteria, but as @debrakidd says, 'not necessarily the lesson objectives' every lesson.

3. Provide scaffolding templates and writing frames.

4. Encourage students to mark their work through peer- and self-assessment.

5. Ensure departmental time regularly includes marking and moderation opportunities with colleagues.

6. Ask your students to curate their own self-assessment task for a forthcoming assessment. Give them a selection of options that include increasing levels of difficulty – so that they feel part of the process.

7. Stop unannounced tests immediately! Why catch students off-guard? It never happens to us (does it?).

8. Regularly moderate within your department; for me that should be once a term.

9. Follow your school's marking code for marking guidance and literacy checks.

10. Choose two or three of your most vulnerable students and mark their books in regular rotation. Do this in class and out of class (with students present).

11. Make use of formative and summative assessment frameworks to secure students' progress. Every child should also have a copy!

12. Try using the yellow box to reduce your workload and pinpoint key marking points (see opposite).

INTELLIGENCE TIP

To identify students' progress and targets, I would strongly recommend you watch *Austin's Butterfly* by Ron Berger. If you have not seen this, it will transform your opinion of feedback as a form of assessment.

Watch the film by scanning this QR code and reflect on the questions below:

- How could you apply this technique in your subject/lesson?

- If any, what are the down sides?

When thinking about assessment, ask yourself the following questions:

1. Are there opportunities for students to improve work for themselves before it is handed in?

2. Is there any curriculum time for students to action any feedback?

3. How close to completion was the feedback given?

4. Does this piece of the student's work form part of a formative-to-summative process?

5. What parts of a piece of work are assessed? What are students expecting?

6. Is marking and assessment student friendly?

7. Has the work been marked for literacy? And is it in line with the school's marking policy?

8. Will the assessment practice support students making progress over time?

9. Can the student demonstrate progress (over time) in their book, i.e. acting on feedback?

If there are any 'no responses' to the above set of questions, you will need to re-think why you are assessing students work.

THE YELLOW BOX

Drawing a yellow highlighted box on the student's piece of work indicates the area you are using to make your improvements to the work which has been assessed. You can use this technique in two ways:

1. Draw a large yellow highlighted box around one section of the work that you will focus your marking on. So if a child has been very weak in the middle section of their essay, for example, you would highlight this section only and mark this part. You can repeat the same action for the vast majority of students in your class, perhaps changing the size or the position of the yellow box based on the students' needs.

2. Draw an empty yellow highlighted box on a blank page next to the piece of work. The scale of the box indicates the amount of work that needs to be re-drafted. You will need to indicate which part of the student's work needs to be redrafted into the empty yellow box.

Techniques such as the yellow box are incredibly powerful for a shift in growth mindset and a re-drafting population of students. By creating a standard feedback action – which could be in a prominent coloured box – you can enable feedback to be embedded across an entire school.

THE NATIONAL PICTURE

Regarding the current debate about life after (national curriculum) levels, we must remember that learning is not linear and that the definition of 'what constitutes a level 5' may not mean the same thing in another subject or another school. There are many concerns about the validity and reliability of such methods.

Past assessment focused solely on achievement and not attainment. The new Progress 8 measure has made some steps forward in focusing on prior attainment and students' starting points, rather than just an end point.

Headteacher Tom Sherrington (@headguruteacher) says that we need a more qualitative approach, with benchmarks that are unconditional and simple to understand for teachers, parents and all students.

MEET & TWEET

Twitter name? @headguruteacher

Name in real life? Tom Sherrington

What's his job? An experienced headteacher who is passionate about curriculum, assessment and teaching and learning.

Specialist topic? His proposals to create an English Baccalaureate framework, as 'a single coherent, unified and inclusive system, catering for students of all abilities' is a real alternative to the EBacc proposals by the DfE.

Why should I follow him? I used to work with Tom. Trust me; you need to follow him!

AUTHENTIC ASSESSMENT AND PROGRESS. KEEPING IT REAL BY @HEADGURUTEACHER

'In practice there are just a few different ways to measure performance from which teachers can make deductions about learning:

Tests: Right and wrong answers or extended answers evaluated for quality. This generates an aggregated score.

Qualitative evaluation of a product against some criteria. A piece of writing, a painting, a piece of design, a performance. These can generate a wide range of outcomes: marks, scores, broad overall grades or levels. Teachers' professional judgement is critical.

Absolute benchmarks: A straight-forward assessment that a student can do something – or can't do it yet. I'd suggest that there is a very limited set of learning goals that are simple enough to be reduced to can do/can't do assessment; in most cases there is a proficiency scale of some kind.'

Read the whole post here:
headguruteacher.com/2014/10/19/authentic-assessment-and-progress-keeping-it-real/

UNDERSTANDING DATA

As a very young teacher, I did not use data. I think this simply stemmed from the fact that I didn't understand it; I was never shown how to use it or told how powerful it could be. It may also be a sign of the times. Twenty years ago, the use of data was never a major topic of conversation for most classroom teachers. The Grim Reaper had only just formed, and inspections came with about six weeks notice and were one week in length.

With hindsight, I was only ever concentrating on being good in the classroom and when I went home, other than dealing with marking, as a 23-year-old I just wanted to have fun and switch off from the relentless pressure of dealing with behaviour. Nowadays, things are different (well, when it comes to data at least). According to the DfE Teachers' Standards guidance, every teacher must 'use relevant data to monitor progress, set targets and plan subsequent lessons'. I have to say, when I first qualified, I could barely remember what a target was, never mind monitoring data! So much has changed in teaching, and I'm not going to say 'it was better back then'; far from it. Teaching is better today; so much better.

The shift for me came in my third year of teaching when I was simply put in a position where I had to get to grips with data. Before this period, the only data I ever came across was levels and GCSE grades for coursework and exams.

Today, when it comes to data, I have never professed to be a mathematician, and getting to grips with the acronyms was an absolute minefield (see page 58 for help on this). To those not in education, it must appear as if we speak another language at times. Today my understanding of data is still not extensive, but I am much more knowledgeable. I know enough to a) enjoy using it, and b) understand it better to inform future actions.

The crucial question is what you do with the data once you understand it. And, are schools attempting to drive up standards by using data to improve teaching and learning?

What follows are my tips for understanding and using data to help you equip yourself and use it more meaningfully.

GET TO GRIPS WITH DATA

It is all very well talking about 'data', but apart from GCSE results and the disappearing SATs and level descriptors, what actually is data for teachers?

Well, data is the information available to you about the students in your class. This sounds rather obvious, I know, but if we expand on this a little more, it includes all sorts of information about an individual:

- prior attainment and achievement (they are not similar; know the difference)
- current predictions and pathways
- projected outcomes and patterns of performance, including group analysis
- the students in your class who receive pupil premium funding
- those students who have special educational needs and a support plan
- those children who have social, emotional and behavioural needs
- those children who are gifted and talented and demand to be stretched
- examination results
- qualitative and quantative information based on your experience of teaching the child, or from the previous teacher.

WHY IS IT VITAL TO UNDERSTAND DATA?

As I said, I barely knew my left from my right shoe on arrival in the workplace, never mind what a grade C or D piece of coursework looked like. So don't worry if you feel the same! It took a couple of years for me to master, and be able to confidently predict, the grading of a piece of work and be spot on with my judgements. Get yourself moderating within your school as soon as possible. Since doing this, I've never had any moderation marks from examiners returned with adjustments made to the grade boundaries.

Why? Because throughout the process I've ensured that I understood both the assessment criteria and the success criteria, in turn ensuring that I understood what was required. Is this a stroke of genius, or the result of astute mentoring and profound judgement? For me it's the latter.

Understanding the assessment criteria
+ Understanding the success criteria
= Understanding data.

In my experience, the vast majority of teachers get it right and should be trusted to make judgements on examinations, levels and coursework. We are subject specialists, after all. But if we have a clear and common framework, we can create (not measure) standards! We can use this information to guide our students towards meeting and achieving the success criteria. As a profession, data has made us feel less and less insecure in the culture of mistrust that has arisen because of external agency scrutiny.

EQUIP YOURSELF

Look at your school systems and software packages for assessment and reporting. Your data manager will probably use a wider variety compared to what you use at the chalkface, but my advice would be to start with the software and systems you use every day and ensure that you can use them to their full potential.

Ask yourself:

- Am I using this software to the best advantage for my students?

- Am I using this software to the best advantage for my teaching?

- Am I using this software to the best advantage for my department?

Consider:

- Are there any components of the software that you feel insecure about?

- How are you using the data to inform your teaching?

- How much of the information is communicated to the students?

I am certain that there will be one or two aspects of the software that you could understand better. Therefore, it is essential that you equip yourself and work smarter. Try to overcome any simple ICT glitches and gremlins in the software to ensure that when you are making any assessment, the process is less frustrating. You could test yourself with another teacher or on another subject's set of data.

WHAT WOULD YOU DO?
Tweet me @TeacherToolkit

OWN THE DATA

As you begin to understand the data and receive confirmation that you are accurate with your assessments, particularly through departmental moderation or external validation, your confidence in owning the data will grow year by year.

To own data even further, you must set out to manipulate it to inform what you need to do. There is a certain level of skill required to be able to tweak data on a spreadsheet or on a piece of software in order to adjust the information to show specific grades, students, results, teaching groups, and key examination questions. You name it, and a great piece of software or a very detailed database can truly allow you to own the data and be the master of all facts and figures.

On the next page is a guide to the most common and most used (and most terrible) acronyms and abbreviations found in education, especially relating to data. Due to the nature of data, this list will probably be out of date by the time this book reaches publication, but it's there in any case!

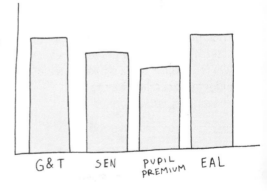

G&T   SEN   PUPIL PREMIUM   EAL

BRAIN-ACHING ACRONYMS

- **A-level** Advanced Level examinations
- **ALIS** A Level Information System
- **Alps** Advanced Level Performance System
- **AQA** Assessment and Qualifications Alliance
- **AWPU(N)** Age Weighted Pupil Unit (Number)
- **BTEC** Business and Technology Education Council
- **C&G** City and Guilds
- **CAF** Common Assessment Framework
- **eCAF** Electronic Common Assessment Framework
- **EAL** English as an Additional Language
- **FFT** Fischer Family Trust (charity that estimates student performance)
- **GCE A** General Certificate of Education Advanced
- **GCE AS** General Certificate of Education Advanced Supplementary
- **GCSE** General Certificate of Secondary Education
- **G&T** Gifted and Talented
- **HESA** Higher Education Statistics Agency
- **IB** International Baccalaureate
- **JCQ** Joint Council for Qualifications

- **KS** Key Stage
- **KS1** Key Stage 1, Years 1–2 (5–7-year-olds)
- **KS2** Key Stage 2, Years 3–6 (7–11-year-olds)
- **KS3** Key Stage 3, Years 7–9 (11–14-year-olds)
- **KS4** Key Stage 4, Years 10–11 (15–16-year-olds)
- **MidYIS** Middle Years Information System
- **NCER** National Consortium of Examination Results
- **NVQ** National Vocational Qualification
- **OCR** Oxford Cambridge and RSA Examinations
- **PANDA** Performance and Assessment
- **PI** Performance Indicator
- **SAR** Self-Assessment Report
- **SAT** Standard Assessment Test
- **SEN** Special Educational Needs
- **SENCO** Special Educational Needs Coordinator
- **SFR** Statistical First Release (DfE data release)
- **UPN** Unique Pupil Number
- **YELLIS** Year 11 Information System

DIFFERENTIATION

You are not expected to differentiate for every child in every lesson. Let me repeat that:

You are not expected to differentiate for every child in every lesson.

It is an impossible task to offer a range of resources for every child every single lesson, but there are strategies that you can embed so that your practice will naturally emerge as embedded differentiation over time. This can only be a good thing for your students and for your marking, planning and teaching.

Top 10 differentiation strategies

1. **Seating plan** As daft and simple as it sounds, a seating plan works wonders. Put every child in a specific location in the room that works best for their learning and for you. Don't be fooled by the child who says, 'I work best next to my friends.' They don't!

2. **Marking books with love and attention** This is the most sophisticated form of differentiation that you can offer your children.

3. **Using data** Keeping a close and careful eye on student data and communicating the information via formative feedback to your students is the best differentiation strategy – after marking – that you can use.

4. **Verbal feedback** Your feedback must be meaningful, sophisticated and tailored to the individual child. A 'well done' or a 'that's very good', is enough to feed their ego, but it's an utter waste of breath on your part and will not help students make any progress whatsoever. Extend the praise comments with pinpointed formative assessment.

5. **Classroom displays** Build up a bank of resources by placing students' completed work immediately on display in your classroom.

6. **Scaffolding** Provide students with a scaffolding writing frame.

7. **Choice of task** Offer at least two choices for everything that you do, with varying difficulty.

8. **Forming and framing questioning** Forming and framing questions is probably my favourite strategy of all! How you ask a question can make all the difference in the classroom. Take a look on my blog for a resource called 'Pose, Pause, Pounce, Bounce'. It will transform your teaching and how you ask students questions.

9. **Students taking the lead** Nominate students to lead a starter or plenary activity.

10. **Students teaching their peers** Challenge students to teach others what they have learnt and assess this by observing the outcome.

MARK, PLAN, TEACH (REPEAT) DIFFERENTIATION

Following the mark, plan, teach (repeat) model of Vitruvian teaching (see page 5), here are a few differentiation suggestions that you can use to help you develop a higher level of intelligence and cognitive thought in your teaching. From just reading and putting into practice some of the ideas below, you will be differentiating by input rather than waiting to react to an output/outcome.

DIFFERENTIATED MARKING

- Just by marking, you will be differentiating your feedback to each and every child. Be wary of time/detail.

- Mark your books, but not every page. Just mark all of them…

- That's all I'm going to say here!

DIFFERENTIATED PLANNING

This aspect of teaching is probably the most difficult and time-consuming for every teacher. You never have enough time as it is, and when you have to start thinking about creating alternative versions of resources for different student abilities and different student needs, minutes and hours can start to ebb away. My advice? Ask for help. Look for alternative resources online, talk to colleagues to see what resources they use, or work with a specialist, for example an EAL teacher or SENCO, to help translate or adapt your resources to suit particular groups. I am always surprised by the wealth of information and expertise that lurks in the different pockets around schools, so get out of your classroom and go and see what other departments can offer you.

- Plan two lesson objectives so that you can pitch work at the correct level for students.

- Use scaffolding resources, templates and handouts – some with, and some without a framework.

- Encourage students to work within different expectations. For example, group A is working on X, group B is working on Y.

INTELLIGENCE TIP

The laziest form of differentiation that exists is going into every lesson, setting a whole class task, waiting for students to produce an outcome, and then simply differentiating a follow-up task or feedback. Avoid this at all costs…

However, in all honesty, occasionally we have to resort to this because we are pulled left, right and centre in a very demanding job with an incredibly high workload.

So instead, aim to move away from this model as you develop your Vitruvian repertoire. As you develop your skills, differentiation planning will become more natural for you and it will take you less time to intelligently plan your provision ahead of each lesson.

DIFFERENTIATED TEACHING

To put it simply, offer a choice. You will be surprised how much happier you feel and how much more harmony you sense in the classroom when there is a choice for learners. We all like choice and we all have choices to make. Always offer different options in every lesson. Allow students to work in different areas of the classroom or on different tasks that suit their preferences. This will help focus your students and will most often lead to better outcomes.

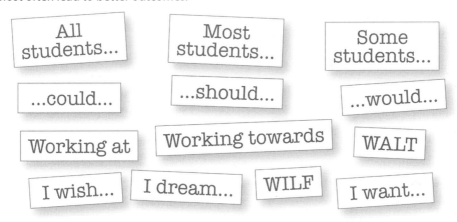

All students... Most students... Some students...
...could... ...should... ...would...
Working at Working towards WALT
I wish... I dream... WILF I want...

Whatever approach you take, it makes no difference if you are still providing students with one simple worksheet. Have at least two versions of the resource or task for different abilities to make expected progress, plus some other options for vulnerable students, including pupil premium and ethnic groups of students who may be identified as under-performing in your school. This can be as simple as referencing assessment criteria on the worksheet, providing a choice or adjusting certain elements of work for specific students. No matter what, always keep the same level of expectation for every child, and teach to the A* grade.

Consistently great Vitruvian teaching requires a deep level of planned pitch. This isn't difficult to achieve, and something subtle such as a directed choice can ensure that students can access classwork and be challenged at the right level.

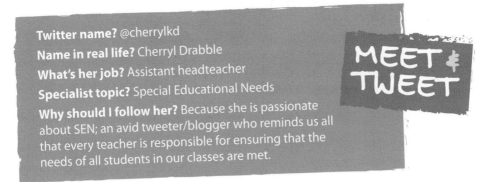

Twitter name? @cherrylkd

Name in real life? Cherryl Drabble

What's her job? Assistant headteacher

Specialist topic? Special Educational Needs

Why should I follow her? Because she is passionate about SEN; an avid tweeter/blogger who reminds us all that every teacher is responsible for ensuring that the needs of all students in our classes are met.

MEET & TWEET

PUPIL PREMIUM

Without getting into a discussion about the pros and cons of the national funding strategy that is desperately needed for all schools in all regions of the country, let me explain the pupil premium.

> 'The pupil premium is additional funding for publicly funded schools in England to raise the attainment of disadvantaged pupils and close the gap between them and their peers.'
> (DfE and Education Funding Agency)

In some of the secondary schools in London that I have worked in, the sum of pupil premium money can exceed £750,000! The school can use this cash to employ more teachers, reduce class sizes, increase targets and interventions for vulnerable groups, or to employ peripatetic teachers who will take students out on enrichment activities and opportunities that they would not be able to access with their own family.

But let's bring it all back to you, the classroom teacher. Which students in your class are pupil premium? What are you doing to support the vision of the school to raise the achievement of disadvantaged students?

The effects of high-quality teaching are magnificent for students from disadvantaged backgrounds; yet another reason to improve and refine your practice.

For you as a teacher to make a difference to the lives of students who are supported by pupil premium funding, you should:

- support students to work independently
- develop students' thinking skills
- provide clear assessments that support learning
- provide scaffolding
- track student data religiously and keep them informed
- make regular contact home
- praise students for excellent attendance
- develop subject knowledge with explicit literacy intervention
- tailor support and resources to specific student needs
- encourage self-study and provide facilities for completing homework in school.

Find out more at:
www.gov.uk/pupil-premium-information-for-schools-and-alternative-provision-settings

HOMEWORK

'Teachers must set homework and plan other out-of-class activities to consolidate and extend the knowledge and understanding pupils have acquired.' (DfE Teachers' Standards)

How far do you agree with the sentences above? Does homework have a high enough priority in your classroom? In your department? Or even in your school?

HOMEWORK: A CONTROVERSIAL TOPIC

I think every teacher goes through a period when they set homework for the sake of the school policy. If you're saying you have never been that person, I don't think you're being honest with yourself! And sadly, every teacher is put in this position when senior leaders try to map strategic methods for setting, collecting, organising and structuring homework across the entire school. Often their plan won't necessarily follow the concept of your lesson planning or the learning that is taking place in the classroom. It makes it hard to set quality homework at the right time if you are constrained by a timetable and bound by a rigorous process monitoring what you are setting each week and recording what the students are bringing back. There is often little time left for tracking what you're marking and the value of it all.

The concept of homework will never disappear.

Whether or not you favour homework, there will always be a time and a place for a student to complete a little bit of extra work beyond the allocated time they have with you in class. Homework can take a bit of a battering from parents, teachers and, of course, students. What parents and teachers get most feisty about with homework, is that it detracts from the time the child has at home to recover and relax or play. But there are other criticisms that give homework a bad name.

The quality of homework set by teachers is a common one – when homework does become a tick box exercise to please school leaders, the quality can deteriorate. I can think of thousands of homework tasks I have set, and they include some horrors: colouring in; drawing a poster; watching the news… I also confess to having followed the one-size-fits-all model using a 'next lesson deadline' suitably timed after the holidays so that they and I might hopefully forget! In almost all these homework activities the response rate has never been 100% unless I have invested a huge amount of time in threatening, chasing, and/or rewarding homework completion. Differentiating homework is not sustainable for the busy classroom teacher.

And then, of course, there is the big question about what facilities and support from family members there may be at home to enable a child to be able to complete their homework in a safe and study-conducive environment.

SOME HOMEWORK NO-NOS

Let's start off with a few things you must **avoid** when it comes to setting homework:

- **Collecting homework at the start of the lesson during the register** Imagine the scenario – all is quiet, all is calm, you're halfway through the register and you discover that Dennis hasn't returned his homework! Stern words follow. Calm atmosphere destroyed.

- **Setting homework as the bell goes or the students are leaving the classroom** Simply, no!

- **Setting a one-size-fits-all homework** You've set the homework, displayed on the whiteboard for all to write in their homework planners. You find yourself scrambling to find an extra minute to write the homework in one child's planner as a) they cannot write quickly enough, b) they cannot read or spell some of your key words – nor remember their definitions and c) half the class have left the room, plus this child's best mate and your next class are already lining up outside. Don't do this!

10 WAYS TO CRACK HOMEWORK

1. **Be different** Homework provides opportunities for students to continue learning at their own pace and provides varying levels of challenge. Set differentiated homework and offer choice. This makes the outcomes even more exciting for you.

2. **Plan ahead** Homework should always be planned, and not a last-ditch attempt to fill lesson time. It should never be used to meet the demands of a curriculum homework timetable or to appease parents. Plan homework with love and attention. If you value the homework, students will too.

3. **Get creative** Homework gives the teacher and the child the opportunity to be creative. Setting homework is all about timing. Setting homework at the start of a lesson gives you the rest of the lesson to clarify any gaps in understanding. Give students open-ended deadlines and offer more freedom for creative responses. Does homework always have to be handed in for the next lesson? Next week? And in one format? Really?

4. **Break down barriers** Homework builds a bridge between home and school. This link can (and should) also be between subjects, teachers and students. Consider linking homework with other subjects across the school, so that medium- and long-term planning are considered in all schemes of work. With careful planning, two teachers can have a two-pronged input that will have a greater impact. Breaking down barriers to learning is why we teach, isn't it?

5. **Consider environmental factors** Not every child will have a home environment conducive to completing homework safely, never mind completing homework to the required standard. However, teacher clarity can make all the difference. If you can build in factors to compensate for poor socio-economic factors and entice students to complete homework while on school premises, bravo!

6. **Feedback** Homework should be marked and students should receive feedback. Do not set homework if you are not going to mark it. And by marking I do not mean tick and flick. Consider setting less homework so that you can mark at a deeper level. By setting a reduced number of homework tasks, you give students time to redraft and act on feedback. Consider alternative ways of feeding back.

7. **Add capacity** Setting methodical homework around your schemes of work adds capacity to the learning process and builds your students' skills repertoire.

8. **Think differently** How can homework involve individuals with their out-of-class-learning? Some of the stigma attached to homework is because it is not seen as adding value. Some view homework as an inconvenience to teachers and think that students have better things to do when at home. Yes, but not if the homework adds value and is thoughtfully planned and assessed. Homework should relate to learning outside of school. Set a wide variety of homework that match your students' needs and interests.

9. **Make homework a valuable commodity** Homework echoes the values of you as a teacher and of the school. Make homework valuable and reward students for hard work completed outside of the classroom. This can be achieved through detailed feedback and meaningful dialogue that encourages the student to complete work and even redraft it. These conversations will instil values that we all aim to inspire in our students. Reward great effort, too.

10. **Be reflective** If you manage to achieve all of the above, homework can offer a further opportunity for students to consolidate what they have or have not learnt. Give students time to complete homework well. Allow them to reflect on their work and self-/peer-assess both in and out of class.

'Unhomework allows the children to lead their learning, as I encourage them to do in the class. My aim is to achieve the position of the guide at the side. In this role, I find they need me less and less as the year progresses.' (Mark Creasy)

Mark Creasy's book Unhomework has a similar idea to my Takeaway homework (see next page). It was amazing that we both discovered each other's ideas at the same time. We were delighted to hear that another teacher felt the same way about setting homework!

Unhomework promotes inspiring, well-thought-out, project-based and differentiated homework that has inspired my own practice. Creasy shuns the traditional methods of setting and chasing homework and rekindles the value of homework, furnishing all primary and secondary teachers with a reliable array of homework tactics, resilience and thought. By testing out his ideas you will secure a classroom experience that lowers teacher workload, yet heightens student grit and independence.

QUICK BOOK REVIEW

TAKEAWAY HOMEWORK

'Takeaway homework' encourages any teacher in the classroom to set challenging, inspiring, differentiated homework that is self-selecting for their students. Offering students a 'menu' of homework options means they can set their own agenda and the teacher can stand back and naturally guide each child to do this for themselves (or gently encourage towards what works best).

This takeaway concept can be applied to anything – for example, staff development, teacher training or action research – by giving staff the option to make informed and professional choices. When you give people a choice, whether students or teachers, you increase their motivation for a task. You give them a sense of freedom; a choice in what they can do, in how they can respond to the task and the chance to return the work to a self-manufactured choice of deadlines. No wonder takeaway homework leaves the students feeling empowered and excited about homework.

Get started with takeaway homework now!

Toolkit essential: takeaway homework

- Write a list of 15–30 homework ideas for a key stage, project or year group.

- Divide these homework ideas into 'starters' – achievable and based on prior knowledge; 'main dishes' – achievable with effort; 'desserts' – difficult to achieve but also enticing to try.

- Add in a few seasonal homework ideas to complete, for example: at Easter, Christmas or over the summer holidays.

- Decide whether to place the homework ideas in a sequential order using a subject-specific assessment criteria. Adding success criteria may remove the exciting aspect of a takeaway, or add incentives to improve, so it's up to you.

- Add a simple statement – no more than a sentence – to describe each homework and what is needed.

- Make sure each homework idea can literally be read there and then, and truly is a 'takeaway', meaning that it requires no further guidance.

- Decide the method you will use to display this – huge banner, tombola, using the interactive whiteboard and a lottery-number selector, laminated and stuck to the wall, as the back of all students' exercise books…?

- Consider setting one random takeaway homework once a half-term (as well as regular homework).

- Consider adding all your takeaway homework tasks to this online fruit machine-style random selector: www.classtools.net/education-games-php/fruit_machine, and allow the machine to choose for each child. Too random? Then let the children decide based on your dastardly and cleverly manipulated homework sheets. Aha: subliminal homework setting with the delusion of choice!

Takeaway homework
Create your own today!

STARTERS MENU

In this area, write a list of 5-10 homework ideas for a key stage, project or year group. The set of homework listed here should be achievable and based on prior knowledge.

Add success criteria; a simple statement describing how each homework will be assessed and what is needed.

Make sure each homework can be read there and then, and works as an instant 'Takeaway'. This means, it requires no further guidance.

MAIN DISH MENU

In this area, write a list of 5-10 homework ideas. The set of homework listed here should be achievable – with effort.

Students will be required to complete additional work, regardless of what has/has not taken place in the classroom.

DESSERT MENU

In this area, write a list of 5-10 homework ideas. The set of homework listed here should be a difficult to achieve, but also enticing to try.

Students will be required to complete a great deal of hard work outside of the classroom. Struggle should be expected, but the rewards should be high.

Assessment/Reward Criteria

This area should include marking and assessment. How will each piece of homework be assessed? This could be displayed with a grading/marking code alongside each homework statement. An indication of timeframe, website links and possible rewards.

Buffet Menu

The buffet menu provides a range of specific choices for some students to choose from providing a more limited choice within the entire menu. The star icon indicates the choices available to them, with instructions provided here.

Menu-o-meter

The Menu-o-meter is the key to explain all the homework available.

A clock icon indicates time task will take (30 mins per clock).

A chili indicates the homework is difficult (3 chillies – very hard!)

The pepper colour indicates the homework is differentiated.

OBSERVATIONS

AS BAD AS IT CAN GET...

When I was in my third year of teacher training, I had my first formal observation with college tutor, Professor Kay Stables. She may have forgotten the observation, but I never have! It was a Key Stage 3 electronics lesson. The objective of the lesson was to get students soldering basic components in order to build a circuit.

Picture the scene. I was all set up with everything I needed: soldering iron? – check; wet sponge? – check; tin solder? – check; clippers? – check; pliers? – check; red and black wire? – check. It was all laid out ready to go for the best demonstration any trainee teacher could ever prepare for.

Do you think it went according to plan?

Of course not! Why? Because I had focused my energies solely on the activities, using my lesson timings as the driver for planning and delivering the lesson.

So, what actually happened in my observation lesson? Unbeknown to me, a student in the second row was feeling rather unwell and was bent over, just in front of the demonstration table. I hadn't even noticed. Without being fully aware of any impending disaster, I started my demonstration. The soldering fumes were oozing, ever so slightly, out of the tip of the soldering iron. Soldering fumes which were sulphurous and could therefore intensify feelings of nausea…

Within a matter of seconds and as soon as I applied the first soldering connection, the fumes of sulphur drifted beyond the first row of observers to the student in the second row who proceeded to projectile vomit, missing all those sitting in the front row and splattering all over the resources on my desk! Yep, all over every component I had carefully laid out and onto the floor beyond, my shoes, the bottom of my trousers, the side pockets of my lab coat, student textbooks, exercise books and even on my spare set of soldering irons!

Cue student hysteria. Cue me, as a very hesitant trainee teacher, heading to the sink to wash my hands. Stage right, enter the design technology technician with a mop and bucket in hand. Stage left, my tutor, while carefully observing, starts ushering students to another part of the room.

And then… I saw the impact of the glower for the first time! (see page 24)

No, not me! My university tutor.

She glowered. What unfolded in front of me was the swiftest clean-up operation you have ever seen! Individual students were tasked with specific jobs. Hysteria turned to calm, and – despite one or two students looking rather pale, covering their nose and mouth – I think we eventually managed to get back to the task!

OBSERVATIONS TODAY

Your first experience of a lesson observation probably occurred during your training on a teaching placement, with feedback typically given on your strengths and weaknesses and how to improve your practice in the future. These observations are often graded against a very detailed and specific range of criteria. From this point onwards, whether it is for appraisal, inspection, CPD or research purposes, observation becomes a constant focus in teachers' professional lives. We dance along to what we have always known.

A CHANGING LANDSCAPE

As I write, the current teaching and learning landscape is shifting on the matter of lesson grading. The challenge for us all, is to move away from one-off classroom performances towards a more sophisticated model of gathering reliable and valid sources of evidence (without a grade) over time.

This change is already in motion and I am certain as a profession we will become more and more adept at reviewing the quality of teaching and learning, not just in a single classroom, but in an entire school over a longer period of time.

There is absolutely no doubt that the Grim Reaper has damaged how we as teachers observe each other in lessons. But as the climate changes and we embark on developing a more subtle process for observing teaching, with a focus on improving teaching, we will reclaim observations for ourselves, making them a positive, enjoyable and invaluable reflection and development tool.

We must make a dramatic move away from summative assessment for observation, towards a model of formative teaching and learning. If we are to truly take advantage of what lesson observation has to offer as a tool for teacher learning, then we need to start thinking outside of the assessment box.

Scan this QR code and watch what motivational speaker Action Jackson has to say about observations.

Follow @Actionjackson for more videos like this!

THE PROBLEMS WITH OBSERVATIONS

In a blog he wrote for me called *Teachers and lesson observations*, Dr Matt O'Leary (@DrMattOLeary), reader in education at Birmingham City University, identifies and discusses 'validity' and 'reliability' in relation to observations:

> *'Validity is generally concerned with the extent to which an assessment samples the skills, knowledge, attitudes and/or other qualities it claims to measure. Reliability is concerned with the consistency, accuracy and replicability of results, but, of course, the two are inextricably linked.*
>
> *The performance element of high-stakes observations inevitably has an effect on the validity and reliability of the observed lesson. Obviously teachers want to perform to the best of their ability as there is often a lot riding on the outcome of these observations. But under such conditions, teachers and students often behave differently, making it difficult to capture an authentic and representative picture of their everyday practice or indeed their real potential. In psychology, this is what is known as the Hawthorne effect: the tendency to perform or perceive differently when one knows they are being observed.'*

In order to effectively use observations we need to overcome the problems that the one-off lesson observation presents, including the fact that it often feels contrived, and is therefore not representative of a teacher's everyday practice. This is why there is such a strong need for all schools and all teachers to develop and and use a coaching model of peer-to-peer observation.

Another problem the old system presents is the subjectivity of an observer. There is an abundance of research evidence that highlights disagreement between observers as to what constitutes 'effective teaching'.

> *'In short, no two observers see the same thing and unwittingly project their own subjective bias into their evaluation of an observed lesson, which in turn casts doubt on the reliability of judgements made as a whole.' (Dr Matt O'Leary)*

The full-time classroom teacher teaches on average around 20 hours per week. They typically teach for 38 weeks, which equates to approximately 760 hours per academic year. For at least two decades, I have been judged and measured on just three (or thereabouts) of these lesson observation-hours, every academic year. So it is interesting to ask these questions:

- What would an observer see if they'd observed my teaching much more regularly?

- What if two observers came along and not just one?

- What if I were part of that process too; what if I could observe my observer?

- What if my observers and I had a tool such as IRIS Connect so that we could all watch footage of me in the classroom? What then?

EQUIPPING YOURSELF FOR OBSERVATIONS

Let us consider a range of reflection questions, written to help you analyse and think about the teaching you are observing or a class you have just taught.

DISCLAIMER

BEFORE YOU CONTINUE:
THESE QUESTIONS ARE FOR TEACHER REFLECTION ONLY.

None of the following questions are to be asked for a 20-minute observation, a one-off observation or a graded lesson observation. If the questions are to be used for observations, then the teacher/observer should consider them as a series of questions to pose within a series of lessons over time.

SUBJECT KNOWLEDGE AND USE OF ASSESSMENT

1. Is understanding checked systematically and effectively to anticipate interventions?

2. Is marking consistently high quality and constructive, ensuring that students make rapid gains?

3. Are key questions asked in order to assess understanding and deepen learning?

4. Do students get thinking time and oral rehearsal?

5. Is literacy assessed regularly, and do students respond to/correct their mistakes?

6. Are there effective alternatives to hands up?

7. Is inquisitiveness encouraged?

TEACHING

1. Do students work harder than the teacher?

2. Can students explain how what they are doing links to what they are expected to learn?

3. Can students articulate what they should be able to do by the end of the lesson?

4. Can students show how what they are doing builds on prior learning?

5. Do students make connections between subjects?

6. Are students inspired?

7. Does the teacher consistently have high expectations for all students?

8. Is every opportunity taken to develop SMSC (social, moral, spiritual and cultural education)?

9. Is intervention sharply focused and matched to the needs of the students?

10. Are teaching assistants involved in planning?

11. Is every opportunity taken to develop literacy and numeracy?

12. Are there a variety of activities, including imaginative ones, to encourage risk-taking?

13. Are clever transitions created between tasks?

PROGRESS

1. Does the teacher build resilience, confidence and engagement?

2. Does the teacher build independence of thought and behaviour?

3. Are objectives rigorous? Do they challenge students?

4. Do students consistently show high levels of engagement?

5. Does the teacher plan for the needs of different groups of learners in the class?

6. Are students making exceptionally high rates of progress over time?

7. Does evidence demonstrate progress of all learners in the lesson?

HOMEWORK

1. Does the teacher offer appropriate, regular feedback that makes a significant contribution to students' learning?

2. Does the teacher set differentiated homework?

3. Do students enjoy homework?

ATTITUDES TO LEARNING

1. Do students demonstrate high levels of engagement, courtesy, collaboration and cooperation?

2. Is praise genuine and purposeful?

3. Is the first hint of off-task behaviour dealt with?

4. Are students given independence and responsibility?

5. Is there evidence of tackling extremism, or at least healthy debates about it?

6. Does learning proceed without interruption?

7. Is behaviour management consistent and systematic?

These questions cover the expectations on you from the Teachers' Standards.

Check them out here: ⟶

PRACTICAL TIPS

It is crucial that we make a move towards collaboration and start to get the most out of observations. Once you have identified your current strengths and development areas, you could try solution-focused questioning, a form of coaching to tease out reflection on developmental areas in more detail.

SOLUTION-FOCUSED QUESTIONING

1. Share your strengths and development areas with your group (no more than three people).

2. Focus on one development area (a strand of teaching rather than an entire category) and describe it in as much detail as you like. How do you currently do this? For example, how do you currently manage Key Stage 4 homework?

3. Encourage your group to ask clarifying questions; for example, how do you follow up on missed homework? The person presenting answers the questions.

4. Ask more probing questions. For example, how do you ensure homework is completed independently? (Try to ask a brief question and avoid giving advice; give the person presenting time to think.)

5. Once you have exhausted meaningful questions, sum up what you have learnt/realised.

FOR THE NEW TEACHER

Observations as a new teacher are, without doubt, incredibly nerve-wracking. They shouldn't be, but they are! Two decades ago, having someone come into your classroom to observe and provide meaningful feedback was an unknown quantity to me. So, how on earth did I survive?

Well, what I managed to do, just like most colleagues, was gather a group of like-minded colleagues around me to support my development: to critique my practice, to call on for support and so forth. I can count a handful of colleagues – some I still keep in touch with today – who were there to provide me with advice on some of the following:

- my tutor group

- my subject

- preparing resources

- dealing with difficult students.

And then, of course there were the colleagues who were there to share stories with, or to sound off to and relax with. It's important to build up a rapport with your colleagues, because at some point you may actually depend on their collegiality in front of students or parents. If you can do this informally as well as formally, and of course at all times professionally, it will keep you much happier in school. So, carry on sharing anecdotes.

Toolkit essential: observations

1. Agree a focus beforehand.

2. Do not do anything different from what you would do day-to-day.

3. Maintain all normal routines and expectations.

4. Keep calm and teach! Do what you do best.

5. Focus on the learning, not the activity.

6. Ensure the students are working harder than you over time.

7. And finally, the feedback. Reflect on the lesson personally before discussing the content with the observer. This is probably more important than the actual observation itself. Feedback should be meaningful and should have an agreed focus before the observation takes place. The focus should be referred to throughout the feedback.

INTELLIGENCE TIP

Teach all of your lessons as if you were being observed. This will ensure nothing changes when anyone else is in the room.

- Remain the same and be constant.

- Make sure your teaching remains calm, focused and of a good standard.

- Encourage your students to continue to learn in the same manner.

- Get you and the students accustomed to extra bodies in the room.

If you can reach this stage, then you are really moving towards an intelligent model of developing yourself the true Vitruvian way. This will encourage a level of resilience in you as you develop throughout your formative years, so that when you are slightly more experienced, you will welcome anyone into your room with open arms. Whoop!

NUMBER ONE piece of advice

I didn't know it as a new teacher, but my number one piece of advice would be to go and observe other colleagues within your department. Start with this and keep it simple. When the time comes, or when you're brave enough, start venturing outside of your department. I still use this advice for myself today. It's the first piece of advice I give to everyone I speak to who is new to the profession.

EMBRACE OBSERVATIONS!

Observations, regardless of what form they take – informal or formal, for development, for appraisal, with judgement, or preferably not – we as teachers should always want to do the following:

- share good practice by being observed and observing.

I can fully understand why teachers may shy away from observations. There may be a multitude of experiences, from bullying to jumping through hoops and from teaching for performance to the opposite end of the spectrum, having been observed for genuine development.

If teachers are wary, there is a danger that poor structures exist within the school, such as weak appraisal and lacklustre staff development. Every teacher can improve. I firmly believe that you can match up certain personalities, or observers with a specific skill set, to work with teachers who are either under-developed or observation shy. This is where the importance of coaching and mentoring comes to the fore. This is discussed in much more detail in section 5 (see page 144).

WHAT TO OBSERVE?

Observations should take the following into account:

- Classroom routines should also be observed and discussed with students.
- Teacher data and tracking of progress over time/Key Stage should be discussed.
- And of course, the observation should be a formative process in which no judgements are offered.

Do not observe another member of staff – or be observed – without a specific focus; make this is a deliberate action. If you do not, it will only leave you baffled, trying to gather all the different sources of information, matching what you see to a specific vocabulary or criteria and preferred teaching style. Remember, as David Didau says, in an observation the aim should be to 'look at' not 'look for' (www.learningspy.co.uk/about-2).

I should not need to tell you that making observation feedback meaningful, is especially important for teachers' feelings of self-efficacy and job satisfaction and that teachers who believe that feedback influences their own teaching, show more commitment to their collective goals.

Introducing IRIS Connect

Software such as IRIS Connect, a video-based professional development tool that empowers teachers to reflect on, analyse and share their own classroom practice, is a perfect example of teachers being able to take back control of what they do in the classroom in order to identify their own improvements.

EMOTIONAL INTELLIGENCE

Emotional intelligence: trust me, you will need it as a teacher. Learn to become emotionally intelligent when working with children, parents, and other teachers.

I have the following questions stuck to my desk at work:

'Can this be discussed face-to-face?'

'Can this wait 24 hours?'

'Is my reply emotionally intelligent?'

The answer to all these questions should be 'yes'! I keep these notes as an aide-memoire throughout the challenges that middle and senior leadership bring. They are equally relevant for situations with students, parents and colleagues alike as a new teacher.

DEVELOPING EMOTIONAL INTELLIGENCE

I have no recollection as to whether or not my emotional intelligence was ever discussed when I was a child. Perhaps that was because I was stable and secure and not a vulnerable child. I have no idea. Did I need to develop my softer side? I certainly have needed to as an adult, and particularly as a teacher. But at what point will these social skills be taught explicitly by you, to your students in school?

In my form tutor chapter (see page 79) I share lots of advice about relationships and how being a form tutor is one of the most important aspects of your role as a teacher. Mentoring students is an incredibly rewarding experience, particularly the pastoral aspects of education where you are in a trusted position to develop the whole child.

I don't need to tell you that within the school, developing a culture of self-regulating behaviour is paramount for all who attend the school – students and teachers. High-quality behaviour for learning is underpinned by relationships, lesson planning and positive reinforcement. As individual teachers, we must develop our emotional consistencies to make a good example for all students. These could be to:

- act respectfully and safely

- model positive behaviour and work hard to build relationships

- be calm and provide an opportunity to put right a behaviour before going through any sanctions

- follow up every time, retain ownership and engage in reflective dialogue with students

- never ignore or walk past students who are behaving badly.

WHAT IS EMOTIONAL INTELLIGENCE?

Emotional intelligence has gone in and out of fashion during my time as a teacher, but I think it is highly underrated. Emotional intelligence is the ability to regulate your own emotions, particularly in challenging circumstances. This could of course apply to you, a colleague, a child or a parent.

A key component of emotional intelligence is self-regulation. 'The term 'self-regulation' refers to the capacity to control one's impulses, both to stop doing something, if needed (even if one wants to continue doing it), and to start doing something, if needed (even if one doesn't want to do it).' (www.toolsofthemind.org)

HOW DO WE TEACH OUR STUDENTS TO SELF-REGULATE?

We first need to teach it to ourselves so that we are equipped to deal with the most difficult situations.

Our everyday lives in the classroom are full of decisions of one sort or another. Most decisions are meaningless but others are very important and this decision-making requires our emotional intelligence when considering the various options, and expressing a preference for one option over another.

> 'KIDS DON'T LEARN FROM PEOPLE THEY DON'T LIKE.'
> Rita Pierson

Imagine a teacher–versus–student confrontation – how do we deal with it? What decisions do we make? There are several key influencing factors:

- our judgement
- our influences
- our attitude towards risk-taking
- our mood
- the student's mood.

All of the above will vary to some extent from one day to the next, but mood is the most susceptible to change and this is the one area we most need to learn to control using our emotional intelligence. This is the area we also need to help the students learn to control. In a confrontation, the emphasis is on outcome. While it is necessary to assess suitable outcomes, it is also important to consider the effects of mood on the cognitive strategies used. We need to think about the reasoning behind our decisions, and what may trigger them.

'Anxiety is generally associated with impaired decision-making.' (Groome, *An introduction to cognitive pschology, processes and disorders*) We generally make the wrong choices when we are stressed or anxious about the possible outcome. This is the same when students are reacting to being told off in class, or when we find ourselves under some additional stress from some of our colleagues.

Remember the list on the previous page:

- model positive behaviour and work hard to build relationships
- be calm and give the opportunity to put right a behaviour before going through any sanctions.

BUILDING RELATIONSHIPS

Working in school, you will soon realise that everything we do is about building a relationship with our students. Students will not work for you if they do not like you. If they don't like you they need to be able to respect you.

I encourage you, if you haven't already, to watch the video of Rita Pierson's inspirational speech, 'Every kid needs a champion.' (www.ted.com/talks/ rita_pierson_every_kid_needs_a_champion?language=en)

I will just quote a small section here that talks about relationships:

> *'James Comer says that no significant learning can occur without a significant relationship. George Washington Carver says all learning is understanding relationships. Everyone in this room has been affected by a teacher or an adult.' (Rita Pierson)*

This is true! We all remember the good teachers; we all remember the bad ones. We particularly remember the teachers we had a great relationship with, whether we were learning or not! However, the teachers that we had the best relationships with were probably the ones that we learnt the most from. Why? Because we had an emotionally intelligent relationship. We were connected with them.

> *'Every child deserves a champion, an adult who will never give up on them, who understands the power of connection, and insists that they become the best that they can possibly be.' (Rita Pierson)*

Toolkit essential: emotional intelligence

So, given that we are working in challenging circumstances, how can we increase our own capacity for emotional intelligence in order to become more resilient in the classroom when things go wrong? How can we individually be self-regulators at all times? (and this does apply to students):

1. Make your expectations known.

2. Give honest feedback.

3. Make sure you offer a choice.

4. Don't tell someone what to do, they decide.

5. Be patient.

6. Help them understand their cues.

7. Allow for small mistakes – that's how we all learn.

8. Say sorry if you have to.

9. Lead by example.

10. Move on!

BEING A FORM TUTOR

Being a form tutor was one of my favourite roles in my formative years. I really miss it! 30 little darlings that you can always call your own; even the ones that drive you utterly mad!

I knew the moment I stepped up to senior leadership I was giving away a significant and important aspect of my role as a teacher – being a form tutor. Of course, tutoring comes with highs and lows, but for me the highlights far outweighed anything else. As the years pass by, I receive a wealth of good news stories from the students I have tutored. Some now have children of their own, are getting married, dealing with bereavement, achieving qualifications and even still asking for references. Seeing the personal development of over 90+ students starting out in secondary school as an 11-year-old can be summed up in one single sentence:

Being a form tutor is about preparing students to become good role models and well-rounded citizens contributing to society.

THE JOYS OF BEING A FORM TUTOR

I would recommend reading the previous three pages before this one, as emotional intelligence is something you're going to need.

All of these problems are yours when you are a form tutor. What would you do to resolve them?

- A new student arrives in your form. Within an hour of her arrival, she has set off the fire alarm. The whole school has to line up in the playground: 1,200 students and 150 staff! You find out that it was this student in your form. What do you say?

- A student has been off for a few days. He returns to class and the social worker informs you, in not so many words, that abuse has happened at home.

- A student has missed senior detention with the headteacher on Saturday morning.

- A parent has emailed you to complain that two other students in the form are bullying their child.

- Some of the students in your class don't want to write down their academic targets in their planners. You know that if you don't say anything, the head of year will see this as a breach of school rules in a millisecond. It's your reputation on the line!

WHAT IS THE FORM TUTOR'S ROLE?

In many situations, you will be the first port of call for a student with a problem or a worry, and in some cases you might be the only person they will turn to, so do not underestimate how important the role of form tutor is. You will need to learn how to adapt your teaching into a pastoral role and to support students with their education at different stages of their physical and mental development. You will learn a huge amount about the physical, social and intellectual development of children in your tutor group just by seeing them five times a week and having conversations with them. Do not underestimate the importance of the role.

As a form tutor you are *in loco parentis* (in place of the parent). You are that child's guardian and, in effect, have pastoral responsibility for their daily life at school.

I am proud to say – even though it makes me cringe at times when I look back – that the three form classes I had (two were for over five years apiece) were a work of art. I invested an incredible amount of time and energy into these groups of students, ensuring that they brought reading books to school every day, represented the school for visitors and interviews, and even at 12 and 13 years old, took turns to bring their pets in from home. You name it, we did it!

But there were occasions when I let myself down, and I at times bordered on being one of the worst form tutors you could ever imagine.

Do not be one of these tutors!

- Feet up on the table and does not move for the entire 15–20 minutes.

- Does not speak to their students. Not one word.

- Provides no context for the day; no references to the media or to the latest news.

- Doesn't even give out tutor notices such as: 'So and so, please go to Mr. McGill at lunch time today to organise the chess competition'.

A form tutor's to do list:

- Provide daily reminders for each and every student day.

- Reinforce the school ethos through everything that you say and do.

- Remind a student to turn up to a detention – this may require four or five reminders leading up to the moment it needs to happen.

- Beg for returns of reply slips.

- Remember all of their birthdays.

- Know the key people at home, every single one of them.

- Find out about their personal interests outside of school.

- Show a degree of being a no-nonsense custodian, but with an air of humour.

INTELLIGENCE TIP

Vitruvian teaching does come at a cost, and it is the most difficult aspect of teaching that you will have to sacrifice. Something that costs nothing, but you have very little of – time! Time to build relationships, time to listen, time to communicate with home, with colleagues… and time out for yourself. Time to reflect, plan and develop. Everything that you do will need time to develop. Learn to manage your workload and the demands placed upon you.

During the silly season in school when academic reports are due, or during the winter when the nights are cold and dark, one could be forgiven for not providing stimulus every morning when meeting students. But I wonder how many teachers do not treat their form tutor time like a lesson at all? These periods of time can last for between 10 and 30 minutes. It's worth having a plan for them, especially if you see students twice a day. I know it is unrealistic to assume that you can plan for this every single day, but it is important to have daily routines in place.

TOP 10 ACTIVITIES TO DO IN A FORM LESSON

1. Hold a tutor group discussion or question time debate.

2. Help organise teams to prepare an assembly, because otherwise you'll probably end up doing it yourself.

3. Silent reading and sometimes structured group reading.

4. Watch a documentary, or read the latest news and discuss it with the class.

5. Complete a whole school or year group activity that has been shared with your colleagues.

6. Provide an opportunity for students to complete homework; after all, some students will either not have done it, or do not have the structured and calm environment at home in which to do so.

7. Hand out letters of praise, rewards, postcards, stickers or chocolates. (Chocolate only just before lunch or after PM registration on the way home. Very important!)

8. Deal with sanctions, have pep talks and remind students of basic expectations and values.

9. Silent observation of peer relationships, particularly the vulnerable and unusually quiet.

10. Administration: signing planners; collecting slips of paper; handing out letters; handing out more letters; sharing virtual learning environment logins and passwords; arranging meetings with parents; watching or taking part in inter-form competitions. You must be a god or goddess at tutor time administration. If you're not, you will be exposed…

SAFEGUARDING

Think about the most needy and vulnerable students in our society (see the pupil premium chapter on page 62). These students may be in your school and even in your form tutor group. This is where we remember why we became teachers. Teaching is much more than just about teaching subjects; it is about the whole child. This is where politicians and government league tables lose sight of the role of the teacher. First and foremost, we are *loco parentis*. Regardless of what the Teachers' Standards say, we have a duty of care to safeguard students' well-being physically, emotionally and socially.

All children, regardless of age or ability, have the right to equal protection from all types of harm or abuse. I can unerringly state, that as a form tutor, safeguarding is the number one priority for all of us. Being a tutor and working in schools with children, is the greatest privilege you can ever have.

Toolkit essential: how t

1. **Great form tutors spend time observing and listening** They invest a great deal of time and energy in building relationships. They have banter or some other kind of interaction with their students, and as a result they pick up on any current issues. They notice things. They are the ones who can save their students from exclusion or from going off-track when the exam season reaches fever pitch.

2. **Great form tutors are regimented** Routines are key to maintaining discipline and relationships and sustaining high standards. A sure way to see what a tutor class is typically like, is to observe how they behave when the form tutor steps out of the room, or on days when the tutor is absent from school. If tutees respond to a cover teacher's instructions first time, or remind the covering teacher that on Tuesdays they always do silent reading, then you know that you're working with a great form tutor.

3. **Great form tutors are the link between home and school** They will help their tutees with various problems, including missing PE kits, late homework, detention disputes or lost locker keys, mobile phones or letters from parents. Sometimes they may need to loan equipment such as pens and pencils (and maybe even money). They will make a phone call home, or send a simple email, text or note in the planner. More importantly, they will often be the first port of call for any child protection issues.

4. **Great form tutors connect the student with other school staff and with other students** They check that planners are completed and signed. They process and record students' awards, detentions, homework and general problems. They will often be seen meeting to mentor their tutees about their school work and progress.

Twitter name? @AndrewHall2015
Name in real life? Andrew Hall
What's his job? Specialist safeguarding consultant and former headteacher
Specialist topic? Helping schools do all they can to keep children safe from harm
Why should I follow him? For up-to-date advice and safeguarding newsletters. He's also excellent at delivery training for teachers, and an ICT whizz!.

MEET & TWEET

e a great form tutor

5. **Great form tutors monitor their tutees' academic and personal progress** They help students organise themselves for whole-school events. They involve themselves! They may even help their tutees take part in a chosen charity event, often sacrificing themselves to do something embarrassing for Children in Need, or Red Nose Day.

6. **Great form tutors make all staff aware** They make important announcements about their tutees in staff briefings, place a piece of work up on the staffroom wall or share a piece of information about a child, whether a bereavement or an academic celebration.

7. **Great form tutors coordinate the way the school can meet their students' needs** They are active in their year group teams and contribute to whole school pastoral planning. They are involved in the small details, feeding back on school planner updates, annual activities and resources that can have an impact on other tutors in all year groups.

8. **Great form tutors are human!** They share the occasional story with their tutees to allow children to gain an insight into their own life. They use real stories to motivate, to sadden and to raise awareness.

9. **Great form tutors have great relationships with every member of the family** They go the extra mile in supporting families and their children throughout school; so much so, that in a difficult situation, the most irate parents are putty in their hands. They break down barriers and follow up on every single action.

10. **Great form tutors have their safeguarding radar on every day** They notice any change in appearance, behaviour or attitude. They keep an eye out for anyone who seems upset, especially quiet – or indeed noisy – and notify the right people at the right time.

STAFFROOM POLITICS

Imagine walking into the staffroom, sitting down on a comfortable soft, spongy chair and taking out a lovingly prepared cheese and ham sandwich from your lunchbox. Mmm! Your teeth are just about to bite into the pristinely cut, triangulated bread; your body is relaxing into the worn out chair fabric… when, from the other side of the staffroom you hear,

'G-eeeet OUT OF MY CHAIR!'

Welcome to the world of staffroom politics…

NAVIGATING THE STAFFROOM

Staffrooms can be a hive of activity, a place of desolation and abandonment, or even a place of confinement and confidentiality. I've also been in some staffrooms where headteachers and school governors have temporarily been banned! But I cannot stress enough the importance of having a staffroom in every school, and for making the effort to get out of your department and spend a break or lunchtime there every so often with colleagues. This is vital for camaraderie and staff well-being. (Just be careful not to sit in the wrong seat.)

Understanding the politics surrounding staffrooms is vital for your survival early on in your career, and something you need to intelligently navigate in order to make the most of them. Do not be intimidated by them. Without question, having a staffroom is an important and fundamental aspect of life for any school, and for you as a teacher.

A smaller school, such as a primary school with perhaps just 10–50 members of staff, will certainly have a staffroom, and this will have significant importance. This will – and should be – the epicentre of your school community.

However, many larger schools, particularly those with new school buildings, have saved space by eliminating the staffroom, opting for department spaces in 'hubs' and 'zones'. Is this a better deal for teachers, particularly new teachers to the profession? No! New teachers must spend time outside of their department to develop as a confident teacher. How do you facilitate this in your school?

WHY GO TO THE STAFFROOM?

- To get away from your own department and escape the departmental politics.

- For a change of scene away from the day-to-day routines.

- To catch up with colleagues for business or pleasure, as otherwise you may not see another colleague for what may seem like an eternity.

- But most importantly, because it's both important and good to talk, and it is an important step towards collaboration (which we will be getting on to later in the book, section 4).

Whether you are new to a job or well established in your current school, you must make the staffroom the hub of all your school life. This will encourage you to be a little more resilient. Are you brave enough to survive outside your classroom and your department?

Now, I know there will be a few staffrooms across the landscape that are divided by politics, pedagogy, accountability and leadership styles, but this is surely temporary and you can change it. You are a cog that makes the larger wheel turn.

The very best staffrooms in schools that I have worked in, or visited, are those that look after their staff – every single one of them. Investors In People accreditation for a school is a sure way of determining how the institution invests in staff performance and development. Keep an eye out for an IIP plaque in the school reception next time you visit a school for an interview. It's one small yet key indicator of good systems in place to not only ensure productivity, but also harmony.

HAPPY OR UNHAPPY?

Signs of a happy staffroom are:

- Teachers organising their own events, such as staff lunches, pub crawls, PTA quiz nights and even holidays together.

- Teachers making cups of tea for each other.

- Jokes and banter.

- Tenderness and caring – teachers huddling in the corner of the room to share personal or professional issues and have private, or confidential conversations.

In an unhappy staffroom, teachers are scared to talk to each other and scared to talk openly within earshot for fear of reprisal. Meanwhile strong characters, such as union representatives or well-established colleagues who have lived and breathed the school for 10–20 or more years can ensure that their opinions are well voiced and heard. This can be stifling for the new teacher in their first five years, unless they are a very confident soul.

KNOWLEDGE IS POWER

There are three types of power: knowledge, financial and position – those in the know, those with the money and those in a position of power to say 'yes or no'. As a classroom teacher, you have one of these Vitruvian powers already: you are a subject expert – you have the knowledge. As a member of staff, you have the knowledge about your school.

One key piece of advice is this: read every policy, blog, handbook, handout and guide as much as you possibly can, and get connected. The informed teacher is well placed in any school. Knowledge is power, so make sure you are well read and well versed.

Teachers love hard-hitting facts. They love hard evidence, and most of all, teachers like others who are generally well read, know their stuff and can express this confidently, whether this is for themselves or on behalf of others. This type of teacher is noticed in staff meetings. This is the person who reads policies and understands the smaller details and the bigger picture. If you follow my advice – and know what, why, how and what if? – you will thank me later!

SURVIVING THE STAFFROOM

In my first five years as a qualified teacher, I worked in several schools and my experience of staffrooms evolved. I soon understood that the teachers were fully in control of the staffroom ethos.

Not all of my staffroom life has been rosy. I have learnt the hard way and had my fingers burnt several times! Most of this was due to lack of knowledge and experience. Here are some staffroom scenarios and how to deal with them:

- Have you ever been in a staffroom with a supply teacher? Go over and say hello.

- Have you never spoken publicly in a staff briefing? There's no time like tomorrow!

- Is there a corner of the staffroom where some staff gather to socialise? Pluck up the courage to go and join in.

- Does the staffroom need a facelift? Why not suggest that at the very least the furniture and displays are rotated every term.

INTELLIGENCE TIP

Get involved with teachers outside your department to form a picture of how things are done beyond your own faculty area. Not just how you mark, or in all things teaching, but to consider what the mood is like across the school. Often this can quickly re-affirm or enlighten your thoughts. Have those mini conversations as you grab a cup of tea! Get out of your classroom and out of your department as much as possible. Make visiting the staffroom a daily occurrence. Some schools insist that you attend staff briefings. Others do not. I say, visit the staffroom as frequently as possible and contribute to your own well-being, as well as the ever-evolving ethos of the school.

#INNOVATIVE

3
INNOVATIVE

'A true Vitruvian teacher is able to connect with their students without the need for jazz hands and performances... whoever might be observing.'

BE INNOVATIVE

So, you've survived a couple of tough years in teaching and consider yourself to be a resilient teacher. You've plied your trade and believe you are working smarter and making intelligent decisions in your teaching practice. Now, it's time to get innovative.

WHAT MAKES AN INNOVATIVE TEACHER?

In the third section of this book, I challenge the reader to consider what comes next? Once you have the basics under your belt, it is time to get creative about the way in which you plan and deliver the curriculum (teach).

Let's assume you can now mark your students' books well, and students actually do what you say (most of the time) and act on your feedback. You've stopped writing detailed lesson plans and you feel that you're now enjoying your teaching. This is a good place to be in, isn't it? It's now time to create your own resources, and it's time to experiment in the classroom. It's time for some innovation.

Definition: innovation

The term 'innovation' derives from the Latin word innovatus, which is the noun form of innovare – to renew or alter. It stems from in – into + novus – new.

WHAT IS THE DEFINITION OF AN INNOVATIVE TEACHER?

Innovation is crucial to the continuing success of any classroom teacher. However, innovation in the classroom does not mean using a new method, idea, product or technological device designed to save energy or time.

Truly innovative teachers are masters of alteration. They can adapt teaching to respond to the strengths and needs of all students; to know when and how to differentiate appropriately, using a secure understanding of what can inhibit their students. This is not necessarily a 'thing' to deploy in your classroom, but a habit. A work ethic in which a teacher views their own teaching as a metamorphosis, a transition towards all students achieving their full potential in their classroom.

Innovation is a true transformation from subject-adverse, to subject-sage; or if not, to a place in which students engage with the learning so that they can connect subject knowledge to the world in which they live. Examinations or not, innovative teachers bring their subject to life and make learning real.

Innovation – however we define it – should be harnessed in schools. We know teachers should be at the cutting edge of pedagogy and practice, and that guidance is always changing. So, a key concern and barrier for teachers achieving innovation, are the bludgeoning changes to our education system – a moral dilemma of sustainability.

Despite the ideology and political interference, however, here are some practical ideas for you to develop innovative practice in your classroom over the coming years.

HOW TO BE AN INNOVATIVE TEACHER

An innovative teacher will:

- **Create inspiring lessons** (most of the time) – interpreting the curriculum to meet the needs of their students and help them access the most difficult content.

- **Create, refine and disseminate great classroom resources** for their students and other colleagues – even better, they may be sharing them with the world (online).

- **Master using technology to enhance learning, not support it**

- **Make real references to cross-curricular learning** and make these opportunities real in their own (and others') classrooms.

- **Establish extra-curricular activities** to support and enhance what they do in the classroom. So much so, that the demand for students to attend the enrichment they are offering is through the roof.

- **Take control of your own CPD destiny!** (TeachMeets, see page 136 are a perfect example.)

- **Film themselves teaching** in order to improve, refine and reflect on their classroom practice.

- **Keep up to date** with the latest developments, academic research and curriculum innovation in their subject.

Innovation in the classroom is NOT:

- Turning on the electricity…
- Teaching using an iPad to a) walk around the classroom b) control the interactive projector.
- Using the latest classroom gimmick, for example, lolly sticks, mini whiteboards.
- Taking students outside the classroom for a one-off lesson.
- Trying 'anything' once because you fancied the idea, or school leadership said so!
- Blogging, using Skype classroom or social media just because you like it.

REALITY CHECK

Before we move on to developing your innovative side, let's take a little breather. I want to share something with you to prove that no one is perfect and to help you feel confident about the fact that things *will* go wrong for you, but that you will pick yourself up and move on.

Here is an inspection report from one of my first observations:

Date of Inspection   08/02/0099 - 12/02/0099

This profile is CONFIDENTIAL and should only be seen by members of the inspection team and the Headteacher of the school. The Headteacher may show the profile to another party if this is necessary for the purpose of allowing the Headteacher to fulfil his/her responsibilities under the Education Acts and the school's Articles of Government.

The profile is provided to assist the Headteacher in the management of the school. It takes no account of the many things teachers do and will not necessarily be a balanced sample of teacher's work. Disciplinary action against any teacher should not be taken on the basis of the profile alone.

This is a copy of information given to the Headteacher in confidence.
It shows a profile of the quality of teaching in lessons seen taught by you.

Teacher's Name	Subject	Year Group	Excellent or very good	Satisfactory or good	Less than satisfactory
R McGill	AR Art	Y08			X
	AR Art	Y12		X	
	DT Design & Technol.	Y11		X	
				2	1

Remember in the introduction to resilience when I said there had been times I thought about jumping ship? This was one of those times. This was in my third year of teaching.

23 years on and look at me now!

TE@CHER TOOLKIT

INSPIRING LESSONS

Innovation does not mean ICT. Innovation means 'to alter or renew'. The use of technology in the classroom can aid the development of learning and help captivate students and inspire them, but true Vitruvian teachers will be able to connect with each of their students with or without the use of ICT, gimmicks or fads. A great teacher will make learning real for each individual in any context. This includes using the basics such as pen and paper and the four walls of your classroom.

Not every lesson should be full of jazz hands and performances – nor would you be able to sustain this level of input – but you should certainly look to develop a routine for developing inspiring lessons as part of your teaching repertoire.

CAPTIVATE ➡ CONNECT ➡ INSPIRE

In your second and third years of teaching, as you gain a level of confidence, you will want to start exploring innovation in your classroom with a level of experimentation and risk. By this I do not mean the latest technology fads or classroom gimmicks; I refer to a genuine desire for self-improvement, coupled with a drive to captivate every single student's attention, inspiring them to connect with you and with your subject.

I'm an experimenter. But experiments work best over a long period of time with a particular focus. For example, I've trialled drawings, using equipment and live-marking in lessons, with students' work displayed under a visualiser and projected onto the classroom whiteboard. This is not something you should just try for one lesson or a series of lessons, but rather something you should really commit to over a sustained period of time so that you can truly be innovative.

The next few pages include a range of strategies and ideas to help you become self-sufficient and innovative in your subject and classroom.

Introducing Carol Dweck

If you are 'not yet' familiar with Carol Dweck's 'Not Yet' assessment strategy, I would advocate using this today! She discusses it in her TED talk 'The Power of Not Yet'. This simple two-word phrase can be used in verbal feedback to a student, or recorded in formative feedback written in a student's exercise book. For example, this is what I would say verbally: 'This a useful overview of the Battle of Britain, but you have 'Not Yet' compared the differences between invasions conducted during the day and night'. By doing this, the teacher is directing the student to focus on the feedback to improve, rather than on a summative grade, with no desire to read or act on the feedback that will enhance their learning.

Watch her TED talk today! www.ted.com/talks/carol_dweck_the_power_of_believing_that_you_can_improve?language=en

CAPTIVATE THEN CONNECT

In order to captivate and connect with your students you need to be able to inspire them. The ideas below are quite straightforward changes, but they can make all the difference.

Top ideas for captivating students

1. **Classroom layout** Change the classroom environment. Produce new and exciting displays; change the layout of the classroom furniture; bring in something from home to inspire and challenge thought. (I told you it was easy!)

2. **Be passionate** Make sure you are excited about what you are teaching. If you are not passionate, why should the student be? You will be 'outed'.

3. **Be clear** Ensure you communicate expectations and boundaries clearly. Praise when needed, sanction where appropriate.

4. **Celebrate progress** Track student progress and allow them to see how each small milestone leads them to the bigger picture. Provide opportunities for success, praise and celebration and consider introducing Carol Dweck's 'not yet' work ethic into your classroom and in your verbal feedback.

5. **Competition** Create a sense of competition once in a while to create opportunities for teamwork.

Top ideas for connecting students

1. **Get to know them** It's a very simple suggestion, but knowing every child's name and something about their personal circumstances makes all the difference.

2. **Offer choice** Give students a sense of control. Always offer them a choice.

3. **Offer variety** As part of the choice, find opportunities for students to work individually, in pairs or in groups. Variety is the key to success.

4. **Offer showcase opportunities** Encourage self-reflection, self-promotion and opportunities for students to speak publicly to showcase their work in front of their peers.

5. **Find out what motivates them** Spend a great deal of time investigating what motivates your students. You will be able to extract all sorts of interesting facts about an individual child when they are taken away from the attention of their peers. One small conversation after the lesson can give you a small nugget of gold to use at a later date.

Another important way to entice your students is through imaginative use of classroom resources. This in turn leads to well-planned, inspiring lessons that you will also enjoy!

Top ideas for creating inspirational resources

1. **Visit teaching websites** Research teaching resources online, including via social media, and pick out ideas that are relevant to you and your students. If you adapt the resources, make sure that you have asked for permission to do so (see page 134).

2. **Take a walk around your school** Every school is a centre of academic excellence. No matter what resource you would like to create, there will be somebody in your school right now who has the expertise to transform your ideas into a stimulating classroom resource. You'll be surprised how many teachers have not walked around their school building. It never ceases to amaze me how often I encounter one member of staff who was last seen in another department several years ago. It would be an interesting idea if CPD leaders arranged training sessions in different departments around the school. This would be a great opportunity for teachers to see how other teachers and departments display resources and artefacts in the classroom. My top tip here, at the risk of stating the obvious, is: 'Get out of your department and go for a walk… today!'

3. **Visit museums and galleries** You could visit museums or galleries as a source of inspiration. Arrange a visit after school hours and take two or three colleagues along with you on a fact-finding mission.

4. **Create a treasure trove out of your junk and recycling** You will be amazed how much junk you have at home that could end up being a treasure in your own classroom. Before you recycle anything and everything, consider creating a space in your house to accumulate things for your classroom projects. Find artefacts at home that can be used to stimulate stories, questions and discussions in the classroom. Collect them together, and once every half-term take them into school. You should also consider placing an advert on your social media timelines, asking your followers to contribute.

5. **Think outside the box** Anywhere and everywhere has the potential to be transformed into a classroom resource. Consider displaying images or text on portable displays, revolving doors, tables, windows or ceilings. Try using digital displays that can be saved and used/updated time and time again.

Now you are a 'resource hero', it is time to plan truly inspirational lessons.

Top tips for inspiring lessons

1. **Start promptly** It doesn't matter what you are doing or where you are, start lessons promptly. That will be my first piece of advice for any lesson.

2. **Starter activity** Students love making a mess, yet they hate spelling tests. Why not combine the two with a covert knowledge activity? Try Snowball! You spell three words. The students write them down. Count 10 seconds while students lob 'snowballs' of paper at one another. Stop. Repeat twice and accumulate nine key words that embed past and present learning. Open up the paper and conduct a brief peer-assessed spellcheck. Or move on and spellcheck later in the lesson.

3. **Plan to stop the clock** Grab yourself an egg-timer and twist the clock to three minutes; allow the ticking sound to be the only noise in the room. Give students a moment of silent reflection to be able to consolidate what they have heard/discussed so far. Ask them to record one question to ask of each other.

4. **Consolidate learning** Look to consolidate learning throughout the lesson. Call it a middle or a review of teaching and learning; whatever it is, plan to review each individual's learning regularly. This is **not** a mini-plenary to simply demonstrate progress in a lesson, but a chance for students to really consolidate learning.

5. **Exit tickets** Exit tickets are a great way for students to feed back to the teacher what they have learnt in the lesson. However, there is little point in asking students to complete these if you never follow up on the information. Plan to include this within the lesson or at the start of the next lesson.

PUTTING IT INTO PRACTICE

- **Visualisers** A great tool for capturing images and videos to project live images on to a screen. A particular favourite strategy of mine, is to ask students to complete a task, then at the same time I do it too under the camera and display this live onto the screen. It is a superb way to capture the students' imaginations.

- **Students as leaders and role models** For example, in resistant material lessons, I have differentiated students by different coloured workshop aprons. This makes an instant visual representation of the progress your students are making in the class. I have tried and tested this over a number of years and at different Key Stages over a long-term design brief. Students become leaders of learning and evolve into the role of a teacher. If this is embedded over time, students start to ask student leaders questions they either should know the answer to, or ask for help when they are reluctant to ask you. Either way, once this is embedded, you must keep a close eye on students moving towards the student leaders for help. The down side of students learning from others, is that this can become all they do, rather than making progress themselves.

- `Data tracking` For one-to-one feedback, group feedback, tracking and motivation, data tracking is incredibly powerful for differentiation and target setting over a series of lessons. Involve the students and encourage them to understand the process.

- `Laptops, mobile phones and handheld devices` I've used them all and have been fortunate to benefit from well-equipped facilities. However, be warned – sometimes ICT can let you down and you will have to resort to traditional, innovative teaching strategies. I have two tips here: a) find out what ICT is reliable, regardless of school infrastructure and b) if all else fails, turn the actual device into a physical object for discussion. For example, 'Let's take a look at this phone. What can we do with this phone now it isn't working?' (Apply discussion to the context of the lesson.)

- `Revitalising and revisiting lessons you have taught before` You may have taught a particular lesson or specific content several times before to different classes, and in your second year and beyond you could probably teach the same content in your sleep, it will be so embedded in your psyche. However, the danger with repetition is that you may lose your spark. Revitalise the way you teach a particular topic by doing it in a totally different way. Mix things up!

Wet and windy Wednesday

It's a wet and windy Wednesday. There is an incredibly high probability that students will arrive to your lesson extremely wild. It is therefore necessary that you adapt your lesson plan to suit the mood of the students and the weather. I am not saying that you should reduce your expectations, but what I am saying is you may have to reduce or alter the timings of your lesson plan and the outcomes that you expect them to achieve. That said, my number one idea would be to have a 5-minute calming-down period at the start of the lesson. This could be a simple breathing or meditation technique to allow students to calm down and settle before the lesson starts.

There is a small possibility that this wet afternoon may lead to thunder and lightning, and if this happens then you're in trouble! Your classrooms and school corridors will echo with children screaming all over the place. No matter what you do or how experienced you are, you will be fighting a losing battle with this one. And what's worse, you cannot plan for something like this. How can you turn this mayhem around? Find your loudest and most engaging YouTube video about your subject – keep the lights on, but turn the volume up!

ICT

Once upon a time I taught on a blackboard; then on an overhead projector. Then, one sunny September day, my department was provided with one interactive whiteboard for six teachers to use. We took turns to book the room! All of a sudden teachers could show what was on their screen to the rest of the students – but we could never book the bloomin' thing. A few years later, a whiteboard appeared in every classroom and transformed teaching overnight, or so we thought…

Fast forward a few more years, and ICT moved even further forward and my teaching was set free. Laptops, handheld devices, visualisers, interactive educational websites, lesson planning tools, Twitter, the technological ability to transfer material between home and school, and so on…

Teaching has become innovative, interactive and truly inspirational!

ICT TODAY

We would be unable to live without ICT resources today. Technology has such a powerful grip on all aspects of school life, and it is now a necessity that all schools and teachers embrace it. It doesn't take me to tell you that the vast majority of our students are far more ICT savvy than the vast majority of teachers – certainly my generation – and that we continue to play catch-up. We live in a technological world; it's what our students know.

The debate today is about the value of interactive whiteboards and other so-called 'edtech'. The million-pound question remains: does ICT add value to learning and student outcomes?

Teaching and learning should be at the heart of what we do in school, and paramount to most decisions we make. For me, ICT holds a vital place in education; it's equally as important as literacy and numeracy. And yes, I believe it adds considerable value to learning and to student outcomes. However, as any experienced teacher will tell you, it doesn't matter what you use or how you use technology in the classroom, the secret is why you are using it and how it is helping students learn and make progress.

Using ICT is no longer external to the curriculum, it is an integral part of computing and coding. How you use technology, and why, can make all the difference in ensuring students make expected progress in this new, vital curriculum area. The knowledge and skills they build will translate into many other subjects across the school. Vitruvian teachers will have to think outside the box if they're teaching computing.

Top 10 ICT tips

contributed by @Shawki_Bakkar_

Here are my top 10 tips (in no order):

1. Get all the technical (time-consuming) parts prepared before the lesson starts.

2. Are all the computers on and logged in? Imagine it took 15 mins for students to get their books out. You are losing valuable time with logging on, switching on etc.

3. Do students need the computers all of the time? Do you actually need ICT resources for this lesson?

4. Is the learning going to be enhanced with the use of ICT, or are you doing it because you have to? Not all DT teachers use machinery every lesson!

5. Are you narrowing the gap? Think about all of your students especially your pupil premium children. How can you support them in and out of the lesson?

6. Do students have the foundation knowledge and skills as expected? What needs to be re-taught if connectivity slows down production?

7. Do students have access at home? Don't shy away from this; remember you may need to differentiate for this, especially for vulnerable groups.

8. How will you feed back to students? Online? On paper? If they do not have access to ICT out of class?

9. How will you show examples of feedback to students to model good practice? And how will students act upon your feedback?

10. What scaffolding techniques can you offer to promote computing/coding literacy? How could you do this?

Twitter name? @ICTmagic

Name in real life? Martin Burrett

What's his job? Primary teacher and speaker

Specialist topic? Burrett is an expert in edtech resources

Why should I follow him? Burrett is not only hilarious, he's an ICT genius and my go-to person for ICT support! He's passionate about teaching and learning, TeachMeets and sharing (great) resources online; he also manages the fabulous @UKEdChat social media forum for UK teachers.

MEET & TWEET

Toolkit essential: the visualiser

The visualiser is a device that projects a live image on to a screen or wall. It may be more suited to visual-based specialist subjects, but I would argue that a visualiser can make a significant impact in any subject and classroom.

- A visualiser is superb for teaching live demonstrations, getting students' work under the camera for feedback there and then and reducing the time between transition and bums on seats.

- It's also fabulous for round-table discussions, when – if fitted for portability – a teacher may come to a particular piece of work in locations dotted around the classroom, and the visualiser can beam back an image of brilliance to the rest of the class via the whiteboard.

- With technology, if students do have a range of portable devices and they are permitted in your classroom, then lucky you – you can transmit any image from your tabletop device to the devices in their hands!

Having worked in a subject where students are constantly on the move, I'm always looking to reduce student movement around the class, but that's not my main aim. My point is that using a visualiser is a tried-and-tested technique that I've used for over two decades, and it is the number one item of technology I still use today. And believe me, this 'live-feedback' technique will never be dated in the classroom. Never!

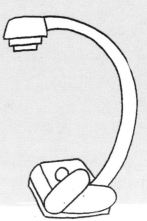

Students, when encouraged, and when the ethos is set, can enjoy and embrace a live demonstration with their peers working under the camera. As a technique, this is a high-risk strategy that will need very secure behaviour management skills and a very strong ethos within your classroom to encourage all students to participate, celebrate and encourage what is going on in the room.

WHEN ICT DOESN'T WORK IN THE CLASSROOM

Having said how fantastic ICT is, I've yet to work in a school where ICT really **drives** the learning, rather than **supports** it. For me, many schools are still too far behind when it comes to technology.

The main reason for this is disappointing. It is usually purely financial and/or to do with strategic leadership. This is an area that is considerably undervalued. As well as due to chasing headlines and moving goalposts, ICT is often shunned in order to meet targets. Some headteachers see ICT infrastructure, as well as devices that constantly become obsolete, as a huge expenditure; quite rightly, considering annual costs can exceed £100,000 in large secondary schools (in London).

However, even schools that invest in their equipment have issues if they don't provide the support. You can have all the fancy kit in the classroom and across the entire school, but if this is not supported by a strong and well-trained IT support network team, as well as a robust infrastructure and systems for trouble-shooting, your ICT equipment will be redundant. The schools I have worked in have all the equipment necessary for any teacher to teach very well – with all the ICT equipment one could ever need – but if the systems are not in place to support it then, as I've mentioned previously, ICT will be supporting, not driving, teaching and learning.

Top considerations for using ICT in your classroom

- **Recurring costs** What are the recurring costs needed to support and maintain the equipment? Often teachers overlook, for example, the annual site licence or the parts that may need replacing, or the software or training that needs to be updated to use the equipment.

- **Training** Whatever you use in the classroom, it is important that training yourself and others features heavily. A school that supports individual knowledge and skills for staff using ICT in their classrooms is a school where I want to work. There's a likelihood that teachers using ICT in the classroom will contribute to learning in the classroom with other colleagues on INSET days.

- **Support** As mentioned above, systems need to be in place to support ICT in your school. If no ICT support is available, there are plenty of websites, teachers on Twitter and blogs that can offer the isolated teacher some help.

INNOVATION TIP

Get plugged in and become Vitruvian today! It doesn't matter whether you teach in several classrooms or you're based in just one, you will find the right piece of ICT equipment that can support your teaching practice, as well as support the learning of all your students. ICT can help you transform traditional methods of teaching a subject, into a more interactive approach, using the ideas that you may already be implementing on paper. **If you use it well, your lessons will fly!**

The essential technology teacher toolkit

A PROJECTOR

WIFI ACCESS

A COMPUTER FOR YOU

AND PREFERABLY ONE FOR EVERY CHILD

DIGITAL CAMERA

VISUALISER

HEAD PHONES

SPEAKERS

IPAD

USB

CLICKER

REMOTE CONTROL

MICROPHONE

BUZZER

INTERACTIVE WHITEBOARD

TIME TO GO CROSS-CURRICULAR

Building cross-curricular links into your planning, teaching and marking can be a very difficult challenge. It is reasonably easy to do it on paper, but trying to address this in your teaching is less straightforward.

At a recent training day in my school, we managed for the first time that I can remember to map every single scheme of work across our entire Key Stage 3 curriculum. As you might imagine, we had produced one of the most powerful documents a school could ever create. In a flash, teachers at the INSET day were able to visually check where other departments would be delivering the same, or similar, content with students at other stages of the year. They could spot the overlaps and gaps, and identify opportunities for refining the curriculum to reduce or omit repetitions of particular topics.

By producing this document, we arrived at something which is only one part of the picture; we have the plans, but not yet the outcomes. It is perhaps something that we could look at to devise these in the future. We will design the curriculum backwards with the intended outcomes clear from the start.

> 'THE QUALITY OF TEACHING AND LEARNING WILL NEVER EXCEED THE QUALITY OF THE CURRICULUM.'
>
> @AlexAtherton100

My current headteacher has instilled in me curriculum values that I had often previously overlooked.

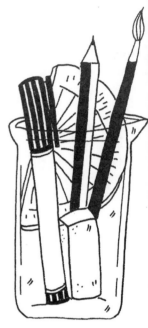

Great schemes of work are the building blocks of any school curriculum. They are not just written; they are taught. Schemes of work are consistent, coherent and have a common goal: to enable students to make progress. Fundamentally supporting all of the curriculum is the assessment structure that lies within it. One cannot exist without the other and certainly the assessment should not drive it.

So how does this affect the classroom teacher, and what part do you play?

Let's split curriculum planning and cross-curricular links into three sections: short-, medium- and long-term planning. In each section I will offer some practical advice on what to do, and what not to do.

Start with your medium-term planning!

Start with your medium-term planning, so you have the building blocks in place, and work backwards if you need to. Cross-check ideas with other departments so that everyone knows what you're doing in your subject area with the students. Once this is in place, you can then start to plan for the long term and work out the short-term opportunities. An online document in one location for everyone to edit is an ideal starting point.

MEDIUM-TERM PLANNING

Medium-term planning may involve projects that will last many weeks. Sometimes planning will be for a 'stop the clock day' when the timetable stops for a day and all students in particular year groups congregate to work on specific knowledge and skills or experiences.

Your medium-term plan should address the balance between subjects, knowledge, and skills and experiences. It needs to consider how the content will be delivered and what the relationship is between different strands of the curriculum. What are the links to ICT, literacy and numeracy? What relationships exist between other subjects? And what extra-curricular opportunities should exist, even if perhaps they are not in the current scheme of work?

Cross-curricular in practice

One of the best examples of a cross-curricular event I've seen working in schools was when students used entrepreneurial skills to design and market a product of their choice using skills they had learnt in their PSHE and business studies lessons. This was all brought together in a 'marketplace' in the school hall, where the entire school, including staff, took turns throughout the day, to experience the design ideas and products first-hand. Supporting businesses and experts were invited to attend, and were there to offer advice and see the process evolve throughout the day. This was a great one-off event for bringing the whole school community together and developing a range of skills that students could use in all of their subjects, and beyond school too.

When you do plan for a cross-curricular day to deal with specific topics, for example sex education or drugs and knife crime, make sure all members of staff support the day. I have seen many performing arts companies deliver these difficult topics to a whole year group, providing students with vital information on some very difficult topics. These days have not been as successful as they might have been because they have not had a structure or the teacher support in place for the topics to subsequently be followed up by other members of staff. If staff do not demonstrate that they value the input of these extra-curricular themes, how can we expect the students to value them?

SHORT-TERM PLANNING

Including any cross-curricular links in a short-term plan, is often left to its own devices. What I mean by this is that often a teacher notes down links to what students are learning in other subjects for the occasional lesson. These may often be haphazard, accidental or following a quick conversation in the staffroom the day before. **This is not short-term planning**. The links need to be mapped out carefully *with* subject leaders and with someone who oversees the curriculum. It cannot be left to off-the-cuff conversations in the staffroom or in the corridors.

More should be done to bring staff together to talk about cross-curricular links. This should never be left just to the heads of department or the teacher responsible for writing the scheme of work. All teachers and all departments should know what the others are doing. In the best of schools this does happen, and with the best pastoral heads of year I have worked with, they also know exactly what is going on in the year group in every department throughout the year. Everyone must know what to expect and when. Everyone, including students and parents.

This will never be achieved with short-term planning, which is why I say:

Start with your medium-term planning!

Toolkit essential: short-term planning document

Consider producing a single-page summary of your short-term cross-curricular planning ideas. These do not necessarily need to be linked to explicit times or dates, but can be a list of ideas with the rationale explained. When the opportunity arises, for example in a staffroom discussion, you will have a document to hand to discuss with other departments. This is particularly useful when your ideas might require taking students out of another class, or impact on the students' daily routines, such as needing to bring in items from home.

Twitter name? @DigitalSisters

Names in real life? Emma and Charlotte Robertson

What's their job? Two sisters, social media lovers and co-founders of Digital Awareness UK. Campaigning to help improve e-safety standards in schools.

Specialist topic? Social media experts!

Why should I follow them? Because they are passionate about informing young people about growing up in an online world, safely.

MEET
TWEET

LONG-TERM PLANNING

Here I am not talking about spending a great deal of time planning one scheme of work. Long-term planning is about planning courses that run over the duration of an academic year, or possibly over a Key Stage. At the time of writing, with the current climate looking at life after levels, schools and teachers have the opportunity to consider longer-term planning in line with curriculum change. This is an epic undertaking for everyone concerned, and is something that cannot be solved in one INSET day. It will require staff working together as a body, in departments and in isolation, to produce, refine and embed short-, medium- and long-term schemes of work. It will need revisiting.

The nature of the school and academic year used to allow teachers to refine schemes of work in the summer term when there was a certain degree of 'gained time' accumulated during the examination period. But this is becoming increasingly rare. There is a much shorter timeframe during the exam period, and many schools are beginning to or are considering starting the new academic year in June or July, rather than in September. There is less time than ever before for teachers to plan long term!

There are some excellent curriculum models thriving in many schools; my advice to you would be to consider the school vision and look to embed your school's values in your subject's scheme of work. If you start from this perspective it will be much easier to refine your long-term planning and build on your school's ethos.

IT'S NOT ALL ABOUT YOUR SUBJECT!

'A teacher must demonstrate an understanding of and take responsibility for promoting high standards of literacy, articulacy and the correct use of standard English, whatever the teacher's specialist subject.'
(DfE Teachers' Standards)

As a newly qualified teacher I had never, ever, considered literacy. I mean, when marking books it was my duty to mark accurately with a focus on spelling, punctuation and grammar, but I had never really considered taking full responsibility for promoting high standards of literacy in everything that I do. Of course, as time has moved on and my practice has refined this is something that I now take very seriously.

I will never forget one time as a young form tutor: the school had set all students a summer homework project, which was to report back on something they had learnt over the summer period. I remember marking one piece of work and came across a spelling of a word that I was unfamiliar with. As a 25-year-old, to have the child's parents question my knowledge of the spelling of a word, and have (what it felt like at the time) my professionalism questioned, really brought home the importance of literacy to me as a teacher. **That lesson has served me well.** Not only do I remember the word distinctly – (gaol/jail) – but I now know the importance of promoting high standards. More importantly, I learnt a lesson very early on in my career, that as a teacher you cannot know everything and that it is much safer to admit that 'you are still learning', rather than pretending that you know everything and that you are always right. Knowledge develops over time for us too!

You may (or may not) be surprised to know that unfortunately in teaching there is a great deal of stereotyping and subject bias, with teachers protecting their subject. I'm not just talking about a teacher saying, 'my subject is better than yours', which does happen, but perhaps sometimes putting a child off studying your subject.

Dare I say that this might be because of a lack of subject understanding on the part of the person saying this, or due to the bias associated with the teacher teaching that subject in their school. Whatever the reason may be, this is dangerous for all involved and you should do all that you can to avoid it. You are undermining your colleagues. You are undermining the collective workforce and values of your school. Worst of all, you may be imparting biased advice to a student.

BUT WHAT HAS THIS GOT TO DO WITH LONG-TERM CROSS-CURRICULAR PLANNING?

Well simply this. If you do not promote colleagues and other subjects within your school, you run the risk of the whole school curriculum being modified so that it does not suit the needs of the students. Remember, we are not in schools for ourselves; our job is to teach students. We often forget this, and it is essential that all teachers and subjects work together for the greater good.

CROSS-CURRICULAR PLANNING = JOB SECURITY

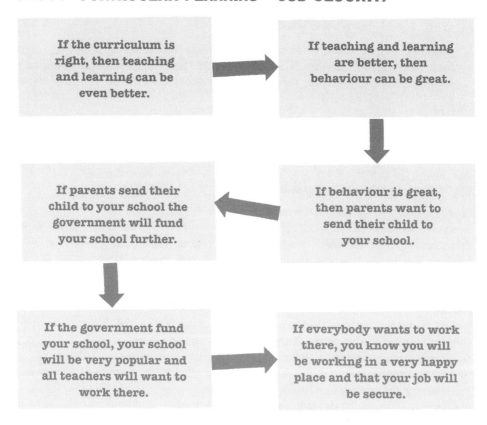

If the curriculum is right, then teaching and learning can be even better.

If teaching and learning are better, then behaviour can be great.

If behaviour is great, then parents want to send their child to your school.

If parents send their child to your school the government will fund your school further.

If the government fund your school, your school will be very popular and all teachers will want to work there.

If everybody wants to work there, you know you will be working in a very happy place and that your job will be secure.

Hopefully now you can understand the importance of long-term planning and getting it right.

Developing cross-curricular links in your subject need not be a difficult challenge. The real challenge lies with the school, which needs to offer teachers the time to plan, time for prioritising and mapping strategically so that building cross-curricular links into lessons, where necessary, is mapped long term. This is something that cannot be left to chance and something that you should take very seriously. If you are not given time for long-term planning, go and ask for it now. Go on, do it!

INNOVATION TIP

There is an excellent paper by Dylan Wiliam produced by the SSAT called 'Principled Curriculum Design.' There is much I could quote from this document, but I have chosen just one small section here to hopefully inspire you to be innovative in your cross-curricular planning:

'...any school was entirely free to teach whatever it wished in addition to the prescribed national curriculum... The real curriculum – the lived daily experience of young people in classrooms – requires the creative input of teachers.'
Dylan Wiliam

Cross-curriculular planning

What do I need to do?

Who do I need to contact/work with?

What resources will I need?

Tweet me your ideas @TeacherToolkit

EXTRA-CURRICULAR

When your teaching is secure and you have become resilient and are working intelligently, this is when you may start wanting to be a little bit more innovative – particularly outside of your department. This may be the time when you consider attending extra-curricular clubs yourself for your own well-being, or setting up your own enrichment activities within your department for students and staff outside your curriculum area. This doesn't always need to be a subject-related activity; it may be something that you are passionate about and you want to share with students in your school, for example, astronomy, chess or something quite unusual and niche, such as capoeira!

> *'A teacher must make a positive contribution to the wider life and ethos of the school.' (DfE Teachers' Standards)*

The times when I have made a positive contribution to the life of the school are the times when I dragged myself away from my department. I've led many girls' and boys' football teams to glory, and also to many cold, wet and muddy football pitches across London. I've taken part in various Duke of Edinburgh Award expeditions, and many overseas trips with the languages and PE departments to places all over Europe.

THE VALUE OF LEADING EXTRA-CURRICULAR ACTIVITIES

There are many reasons to lead extra-curricular activities, and the different types of activities you choose can have different outcomes for both the students and yourself.

The extra-curricular activities can:

- help build relationships with the students

- help break down barriers between teacher and student

- help you as a teacher to see another aspect of the school life

- enable downtime for the students to relax/switch off

- develop another side of a student's skillset beyond academia
- enhance students' academic ability
- promote the value of scholarship
- help build great teamwork skills
- help develop the whole child
- enable students and teachers alike to make wider contributions to school life
- take away the pressure of the curriculum, but also discreetly enhance it
- take away the pressure of anything stipulated by the school
- promote positive behaviour.

Start a club now!

- Chess club
- Board games club
- School radio
- School newspaper
- Manager of (insert sport here) team
- Astronomy club
- Book club
- Wildlife and the environment club
- Gardening club
- Film club

- STEM: 3D printing, robotics, coding and engineering
- Debating society
- School council
- Art club
- Photography club
- Music groups
- Drama club
- DofE Award or cadets/scouts
- Rock choir
- Baking group

CONTINUING PROFESSIONAL DEVELOPMENT

This is probably one of my favourite topics in this entire book. I've always been a reflective teacher, but since leading whole school CPD for the past eight or nine years, I have started to take professional development incredibly seriously. I mean this from a personal point of view in my own practice, not just as a responsibility given to me to lead others.

I have placed this chapter in the 'innovative' section of the book because once you are secure in your own teaching, you will be in a much more confident position to start thinking about your own professional development. This will vary according to your own needs and your role within the school and will require some thought. Not all teachers consider their own professional development a priority. I don't mean only the teachers nearing the end of their career, but relatively new teachers too. Perhaps this is because of a lack of CPD opportunities within their school, but the danger is that they could become disaffected. CPD is important for teacher well-being.

TAKE CONTROL

It is important that you are innovative with your own professional development. Sadly, not all schools will support you in what you want to do and there could be a dichotomy between the needs of the school versus the needs of your department, and then your own needs. To take full control, I have taken CPD into my own hands; reflecting regularly online in my own teaching blog, @TeacherToolkit. This has seen my own reflections enhance and evolve as my readership has grown to over 1 million readers per year. As the demand to read my blogs has increased, I have seen the need for me to reflect on every aspect of school life and everything I do.

Although I've always remained clear that I do this for my own professional development, feedback on my blog has shown that it has enhanced many, many others' CPD across the world. This is a small example of how CPD can start from an innovative approach and have an incredible impact on your own (and many others') professional classroom practice.

> 'POWERFUL PROFESSIONAL DEVELOPMENT HELPS CHILDREN SUCCEED AND TEACHERS THRIVE.'
>
> David Weston, CEO of the Teacher Development Trust

REFLECT

It is vital that schools, school leaders and individual teachers grasp control of their own professional development with two hands. Consider these reflective questions:

1. What does good CPD look like in schools? What does it look like in your school?

2. What does good CPD look like for you? How do you know? Where is the evidence?

3. How does this CPD help your students?

4. What follow-up support is offered as a result of the CPD offered/attended?

5. What/Why/How/When do you evaluate the impact of CPD on your own classroom practice?

> 'A TEACHER MUST REFLECT SYSTEMATICALLY ON THE EFFECTIVENESS OF LESSONS AND APPROACHES TO TEACHING.'
>
> DfE Teachers' Standards

By reflecting on 'effective CPD', teachers could:

1. Develop a shared responsibility for CPD and teaching and learning.

2. Sustain their own professional development so that it becomes an ongoing process.

3. Regularly evaluate the impact CPD has on their students.

4. Support each other and one another's professional development, including observing each other much more frequently.

5. Back CPD up with research, innovation, and evidence – but not always.

6. Scan this QR code for Developing Great Teachers - Academic Research by The Teacher Development Trust

SUBJECT KNOWLEDGE

Subject knowledge is covered in more detail in 'Refining your practice' (see page 118). Here I will touch on the requirement for CPD in your subject area only.

> '*A teacher must have a secure knowledge of the relevant subject(s) and curriculum areas, foster and maintain pupils' interest in the subject, and address misunderstandings.*' (*DfE Teachers' Standards*)

You cannot achieve this based on a degree that you achieved five years ago. You secure knowledge in your subject as you experience teaching the subject, and as you interpret the curriculum and the assessment framework with the students in front of you. Theory cannot be applied without practical experience. Each of these influences will feed into who you are and how you teach. They will also inform your CPD needs, and if they don't, somebody else will probably tell you!

WHAT DOES GOOD CPD LOOK LIKE?

For me, one-off CPD events make little impact on teachers, regardless of any school priorities, unless they are engaging, inspiring and, above all, meaningful to individual teaching practice. There must be an opportunity for consolidation and a time to revisit this CPD in the future. If there is nothing planned for reflection, then there has been no forward thinking on the part of the CPD provider and no time set aside for the teachers to evaluate the impact of the training. CPD must be useful in the classroom the very next day!

I've attended and sat through many INSET days myself – far more than I can remember. I've also planned and led hundreds of them. Of the most inspiring days I've been lucky enough to attend, 99% have been in-house with my colleagues. The most empowering ones of all have been led by my closest colleagues themselves.

After 20 years, I can probably count on just my two hands the total number of CPD events where the CPD has made an impact on me personally. That equates to, on average, one measly and uplifting training day every other year for the entire time I've been teaching. This is simply not good enough!

'The standard model of teacher professional development is based on the idea that teachers lack important knowledge... The result has been teachers who are more knowledgeable, but no more effective in practice.'
(Dylan Wiliam)

WHY REVIEW CPD?

In recent years, a number of consultations have reported that opportunities for teachers in England:

- 'are insufficiently evidence-based

- do not focus sufficiently on specific student needs

- are too inconsistent in quality

- lag behind those experienced by colleagues elsewhere internationally'.

(Developing Great Teaching Summary – see QR code on page 111.)

'A TEACHER MUST TAKE RESPONSIBILITY FOR IMPROVING TEACHING THROUGH APPROPRIATE PROFESSIONAL DEVELOPMENT, RESPONDING TO ADVICE AND FEEDBACK FROM COLLEAGUES.'

DfE Teachers' Standards

Toolkit essential: CPD

Here are some of my best ideas for individual teachers engaging with their own professional development.

1. Attend a TeachMeet (see page 136).

2. Join Twitter and/or Facebook groups to connect with like-minded individuals who teach your subject. I only wish I had had Twitter in 1997 – ooh, the things I would have learnt and the bad practice I would have dismissed much more quickly.

3. Join your subject professional society. For example, I belong to DATA – Design and Technology Association, and ASCL – Association of Schools and College Leaders. I've received monthly publications which have helped me keep up to date with national news, and I've also connected with colleagues far beyond my own institution. Over time, I have been able to contribute to both publications and have had my own – and my school's – classroom practice shared nationally.

4. Allocate adequate time to engage with professional development. One day is never enough to embed anything.

5. Take the time to participate in something meaningful for your own development outside of school, obviously balancing this with your school priorities. For example, this may be a Masters degree – something that you can commit to over a longer period of time that will benefit you professionally as well as your school.

6. Schools with outstanding professional development models encourage tailored CPD pathways for the individual teacher. Consider committing yourself to a variety of options, both inside and outside your department, in addition to your direct day-to-day responsibilities.

HOW TO PLAN EFFECTIVE CPD FOR YOU/YOUR SCHOOL

INSET days and CPD sessions shouldn't just be a random selection of events, but should be a series of focused, prioritised and effective opportunities for individuals, teams and the school. If you are either planning an INSET day for others, or taking part in an INSET day yourself, you should consider looking at the bigger picture.

- It is important to remember, first and foremost, that professional development must be about helping teachers teach better so that students can learn and make progress. What is the key learning (for staff) that you hope to achieve in the session?

- You must consider at an early point what you expect the teachers or staff to produce as an outcome of the day. It could be new programmes of study, schemes of work, lesson plans, new learning protocols, new lesson protocols… the list is endless. What would be the best way for teachers to capture their learning in a way that will help them enhance the outcomes for students (and each other)?

- An area often overlooked is the well-being of those participating in the event. Think about how staff will learn best – through big questions, high-quality input, opportunity for collaborative or cooperative learning…? Outstanding professional development has a combination of presentations or input, an opportunity to chat and discuss the learning, some time to think and reflect and regular breaks to allow staff to discuss and socially construct meaning together. On some days, an element of differentiation can work well, by offering a choice of sessions to meet the needs of different staff. This needs to be carefully designed into the structure.

COMMON CPD PITFALLS AND SOLUTIONS

…if you find yourself in the position of leading CPD for others.

1. **Do not read from a PowerPoint slideshow** We've all encountered this. Despite the experience, we may have even done it ourselves to ease the nerves. 'Information giving' is identified as the top hate by all who attend any type of training, in or out of school.

   Possible solution Provide the handouts for staff to read in advance. If this is not possible, offer short periods throughout the day to digest the information and discuss issues with colleagues or the speaker. Then, in your presentation, just focus on the key information. This will ensure prompt delivery and keep the audience's interest and focus. You will connect more with the audience and will be able to add in humour and evidence.

2. **Do not go through housekeeping information at the start of a session** Introductions, housekeeping and fire alarm drills are necessary, but not essential, and by far the second worst part of any training event. Such information should be kept well away from the true purpose of the day.

   Possible solution Give all housekeeping information and introductions on a printed agenda to all attendees and display the information on screen as colleagues are arriving to take their seats.

3. **Do not go past the published finishing time** I believe every agenda can be succinct and brief. Finishing slightly before the allotted time will ensure staff leave happy. Do not plan too much content in your session, or let questions, last-minute announcements and discussions make your session run over.

   Possible solution Invite questions just before a final coffee break, and wherever possible respond to the individual rather than the whole audience, by asking that member of staff to speak with you during the break. This way you will minimise the number of questions that warrant a whole-audience set of ears. Alternatively, pre-empt questions by displaying key messages on a projector screen or by providing an additional FAQs handout as staff enter or leave the room.

4. **Do not allow a training event to be hijacked by staff meetings** When staff come together in-house, the purpose of any gathering should be clear. Meetings should be kept securely within the 1,265 directed time of all school calendars and used for information-giving and coming together of groups of staff. INSET days should remain protected for their original intention – staff training. Do not allow staff meetings to creep into training days, ever!

Possible solution Make sure there is a distinct format for your training event and specify what staff will do when gathered, and what they will be receiving as part of their development. Plan a series of workshops staff can lead and opt in or out of, ensuring a range of activities to provide choice and flexibility throughout the day.

5. **Do not forget your practical preparations** We have all sat in a room feeling far too hot – or even too cold. Such simple external factors can mean the difference between a good and bad experience. It is vital that a CPD leader considers the room and the user experience of those attending. Review external noise, wonky projectors, screen displays and video resources that could possibly fail on the day. Also consider table layouts, font size, dried-out board markers, loud banging doors and the need for a microphone for those who cannot project their voice in a large room.

Possible solution Double-check and triple-check; have a back-up plan just in case!

6. **Do not rely on poor-quality video clips** Perhaps a particular clip is inspiring; maybe even relevant for that one key point you wish to address throughout the day, but those speaking should ensure thorough research in this area. In a world of social media, there is ever more material available to us, probably far too much. Search around, look for video content that avoids mindless advertising, poor sound quality and hand-held amateur footage.

Possible solution Do your research. Make sure any video content is relevant, inspiring and succinct. Ask ICT staff to help you convert your chosen footage into a document file saved on your computer or memory stick so that: a) you know the file will still exist on the day; b) you can ensure there will be no inappropriate advertising; c) you can avoid any possible connectivity issues on the day.

7. **Do not succumb to acronym culture** As teachers, acronyms are a part of our everyday life: DfE, HMI, SEF, EAL, TA, CPD… and the list goes on. There are thousands of school acronyms up and down the country, some school-specific, some even department-specific. I'm not a cynic, but please spare us from anything new. There is no need to devise a new acronym for every new school action plan.

Possible solution It is possible to make an idea seem new and innovative without a new acronym. Make your ideas stand out by creating a distinctive logo or by using a funky font or colour. If the topic you are covering on a training day happens to have a load of new government acronyms associated with it, then prepare a list of the acronyms on a handout for your audience to refer to, and use them sparingly and sensitively in your presentation.

MEET AND TWEET CPD!

I tweeted the following question to some of the teachers I connect with online, and this is what they replied to me within 140 characters!

Question: Name the one 'CPD thing' that has had significant impact on you professionally over a sustained period.

BEING A MEMBER OF A PROFESSIONAL SUBJECT ASSOCIATION OFFERING JOURNALS AND COURSES AND NETWORKING - BOTH NATE AND NATD WERE INVALUABLE.

@DebraKidd

WHAT REALLY OPENED MY EYES WAS LEARNING WHAT IT MEANS TO HAVE A VISION IN EDUCATION - ASKING THE IMPORTANT QUESTION OF WHY WE DO WHAT WE DO.

@IMissChalk

LEVERAGE LEADERSHIP - 10MIN WEEKLY OBSERVATIONS WITH 1 HIGH LEVERAGE ACTION STEP GIVEN. FEEDBACK, MODEL AND PRACTICE UNTIL YOU GET RIGHT!

@Benita_Simmons

UNDERTAKING A MASTERS & CONTINUING WITH RESEARCH. THE WORK OF SCHOOLS SHOULD BE ROOTED IN EVIDENCE. TOO MUCH IS OFTEN DONE WITHOUT IT!

@RobCampbe11

THE OPPORTUNITY TO PLAN AND DELIVER CPD WITH MANY DIFFERENT COLLEAGUES. I LEARN FROM LEADING THE EVENT AND FROM THOSE I WORK WITH.

@ASTSupportAAli

THE ONLY CPD WHICH HAS HAD ANY LASTING IMPACT WAS MY PGCE. IT DIDN'T TEACH ME HOW TO DO EVERYTHING, BUT IT SHOWED ME HOW TO KEEP TRYING.

@DisIdealist

@SLTCHAT ON A SUNDAY EVENING IS REALLY USEFUL TO GENERATE AND SHARE IDEAS ON A REGULAR BASIS WITH IDEAS FROM A LARGE NUMBER OF COLLEAGUES.

@SSGill76

@FUTURELEADERSCT & FOUNDATIONS TRAINING FOR HEADSHIP. BECAME HT WITHIN YEAR OF STARTING. CONTINUES TO SUSTAIN & INSPIRE WITH ONGOING SUPPORT.

@TGriffiths123

ATTENDING TEACHMEETS HAS EXPANDED MY HORIZON ON TOOLS AND SKILLS AVAILABLE TO ME AND ALSO THE WEALTH OF RELATIONSHIPS WITHIN UK EDUCATION.

@ActionJackson

WORKING BESIDE AN EXPERIENCE PRACTITIONER IN A SEMI OPEN PLAN ENVIRONMENT WHEN YOU WERE CONSTANTLY LEARNING AND BEING OBSERVED. TEAM WORKS.

@RehanaShanks

I DID A POST GRAD CERT IN TEACHING EAL - THIS HAS HAD MOST IMPACT ON MY PRACTICE WITHOUT A DOUBT.

@HeyMissSmith

READING & WRITING BLOGS, DEBATING IDEAS ON TWITTER, TRYING THEM OUT IN THE CLASSROOM.

@Informed_Edu

AN IMPROVISATION COURSE I WENT ON 20 YEARS AGO INFLUENCES ME TO THIS DAY - WE WERE TREATED AS 'STUDENTS' & 'DID' THE LESSON - VERY POWERFUL.

@Sue_Cowley

CHILD PROTECTION TRAINING HAS HAD A HUGE INFLUENCE ON ME. I NOW KNOW WHAT TO DO IF AND WHEN A CHILD MAKES A DISCLOSURE AND WHAT TO LOOK FOR.

@NancyGedge

REFINING YOUR PRACTICE

The art of teaching can be likened to the art of buying a new bed: there are many different styles out there and you have to choose the one that is right for you; you have to consider the different mattresses and try them out to see how they suit your height, weight, sleeping style… This is no quick decision. It will take a lot of time testing, evaluating and reflecting. And of course, the bed and mattress that suits you aged 20 will not necessarily be the same one that suits you aged 40.

With teaching, there is no single ideal teaching method, or pedagogy, and your teaching should constantly be readjusted, refined and evaluated. Just as the intake and cohort of your students evolve, so should your teaching methods. I'm not the same teacher I was 20 years ago. I am certainly not the same teacher I was last year. I'm constantly refining what I do and evaluating my practice.

My thoughts on teaching and learning have shifted significantly over the past 3–5 years. More so, because I have been leading on teaching and learning for other teachers. Being in such a privileged position as this, means that I need to ensure that I am at the forefront of best practice, bringing teachers along with me and I with them…

HOW DO WE REFINE PRACTICE?

Refining practice is about the small details. From my point if view, this is all about becoming more and more reflective, and is something we consider as a key element of Vitruvian teaching in the next section (see page 127). I cannot stress enough that the best CPD you can have is visiting other schools and observing other teachers in and out of your school.

Ideally, all schools should put in place a mechanism so that you can observe yourself. There are many solutions out there, and it will fundamentally be down to your school to put a robust and meaningful system in place. However, if you're feeling isolated and that this is impossible to achieve, you can buy an inexpensive camcorder online.

> 'THE BEST WAY TO REFINE YOUR PRACTICE IS BY BEING AN OBSERVER OF OTHER TEACHERS AND YOURSELF.'
>
> @TeacherToolkit

Thoughts on lesson observations #1: The surgeon and the scalpel

In this inspirational blog, former HMI Roy Blatchford discusses lesson observations from the perspective of the observer.

'A few years ago I lay on a surgeon's table, under local anaesthetic, to have a benign melanoma removed from my wrist. The lead surgeon began cutting precisely then passed over the scalpel to one of his juniors. Within thirty seconds he seized it back, clearly not content with the direction of the incision. He at once offered both the junior and me some reassuring words.

It struck me then – it was in my early days of being an HMI – that my observing a lesson was of little use to the teacher if all I did was to offer some comments once the pupils had left the classroom. I would not have wanted the surgeon to let his junior go on cutting in the wrong direction, saving the feedback to later. My wrist is too precious to me for that.

Ever since that moment under the knife, formal inspection apart, I have rarely observed a lesson without interacting in some way.'

Roy Blatchford, Director of the National Education Trust

Would you intervene? If you saw any lesson developing down a path you thought was not part of the plan, or that 'learning' appeared to be lost, would you step in? And how and when would you do so? To be able to do this, and to do it well, is a fine skill requiring a wide range of knowledge and experience. If the intervention is delivered poorly or mistimed, there can be harmful consequences – an undermining of professionalism and perhaps 'losing face' in front of students. But, if it is handled well it can be of great benefit to the teacher and students alike.

QUICK BLOG REVIEW

When I read Roy Blatchford's blog, it happened to coincide with me observing a colleague at work through video technology, and for the first time using in-ear coaching live in the lesson, offering instant feedback for the teacher to act on. In many ways, this was the surgeon's scalpel. I was stopping the teacher from going in the wrong direction, providing feedback there and then.

Observing from a distance like this, I was able to direct, probe and question throughout the observation, speaking to the teacher via a small, discreet headphone outside of the classroom. The purpose was to help the teacher clarify misconceptions and general snippets of behaviour or learning they may have missed. For the first time, I realised I was able to help the teacher **make the correct incision at the right time**. It was a transformational moment for me after 20 years of observing other teachers in classrooms.

No sooner had we finished, we discussed the content and watched the footage of the lesson together. Watching the lesson unfold, the points where I had intervened to support and challenge were incisive and obvious. Together, we discussed the lesson in detail and used the software to record questions, prompts and feedback. Sadly, the software was unable to record my own coaching and mentoring prompts, but it was then I suddenly realised that this was yet another missed opportunity; for potential (new) observers to watch the observer offer feedback in a coaching role (or at least listen to my comments).

How incredible, perhaps transformational, in anyone's professional development would it be for them to observe the observer making an incision (in the lesson)? Should we make this happen more often so that we are not working in silos? Should schools be working much harder to establish triad-observation groups so that staff are free to observe each other observing? I think we all should be aiming for this.

Consider the following…

1. At what point do we continue to take risks, balanced against the desire to cease experimentation?

2. At what point should the lead surgeon (the observer) take over the scalpel to stop the teacher going in the wrong direction?

3. How often have you been the observer in a lesson observation and intervened with students/the teacher?

4. If you have intervened, what was the impact/outcome? How was the intervention received?

5. How can schools establish a model **where teachers can watch the observer observing** and provide incisive feedback before, during and after the lesson?

WHAT CAN YOU DO?

THINK ABOUT

- When did you last watch another teacher teach a lesson?
- Did you go back to observe them again?
- What did you learn from this experience?
- What feedback could you provide?
- What time have you given this teacher to act on your feedback?
- Have you revisited this?

MORE IMPORTANTLY

- When did you last watch yourself teach?
- When did you last reflect on your classroom practice with hard evidence?

Remember: the best way to refine your practice is by being an observer of other teachers and yourself.

QUESTIONS FOR REFLECTION

Teaching

1. Do you consistently have high expectations for all students?
2. Is intervention sharply focused and matched to the needs of the students?
3. Do you create transitions between tasks?
4. How do you know when to speak and when to pause?
5. How do you use body language and hand signals to follow up instructions?
6. Do you use any subtle gestures to encourage students to engage?

Behaviour

1. Is the first hint of off-task behaviour dealt with?
2. How do you approach eating in class?
3. Is any form of teacher reprimand escalated by other students in the class?
4. Is your approach to behaviour management consistent and systematic?
5. How do you continue a lesson after a disruption, without creating a further focus on the primary behaviour?

Attitudes to learning

1. Do students demonstrate high levels of engagement, courtesy, collaboration and cooperation?
2. Is praise genuine and purposeful?
3. Are students given independence and responsibility?
4. Does learning proceed without interruption?

You can only understand and answer these questions and let them help you refine your practice if you become an observer – whether this is observing somebody else or yourself. Finding the answers to these questions can be facilitated through coaching and mentoring (see page 144). And if you ever have the chance to become a mentor for somebody else, grab it with both hands! It is incredible CPD in your second or third year of teaching. However, be warned. You must have all the basics in place, and be sure your school is supporting you, before being able to master observing colleagues and providing meaningful/difficult feedback.

INNOVATION TIP

Grab that video camera and film yourself today. You won't regret it… Only the hardiest, most resilient and reflective teachers are truly innovative in proactively filming their own practice and analysing their teaching. This is one of the most innovative ways you can help yourself grow and improve. If I could have my way, video self-analysis would be compulsory, and I would introduce it within the Teachers' Standards.

KEEPING UP TO DATE

Whatever route you take into teaching, remember that you bring a wealth of knowledge and skills with you into the classroom to impart a love of learning to your students.

It can be easy to forget this during your first few years, as you spend your time mastering the art of teaching and the techniques required to deal with complex and dynamic situations when managing the classroom. But with a little effort you can combine those classroom skills with the subject knowledge you have gained in your degree to the great benefit of your students.

'All teachers must demonstrate a critical understanding of developments in the subject and curriculum areas, and promote the value of scholarship.' (DfE Teachers' Standards)

Whether in their first or their 40th year of teaching, every teacher has a responsibility to keep up to speed with subject knowledge, curriculum and assessment changes, examination criteria and the latest advances in academic research.

Teachers in general, though, particularly newly qualified teachers and those in their early years, will be so pushed for time, that they will barely get a chance to read material in school. This will be even harder out of school when all most teachers want to do is slob on the sofa and crack open a bottle!

As I have said before, it is much easier today than it was 20 years ago. At the click of a button, I can now share student work and allow teachers across the world to see this and receive instant feedback. This was unheard of a decade ago. Through social media it is even easier to keep up with your subject developments. But it is also even more important to keep up to date in general – education is moving much more quickly than it used to.

With this in mind, this chapter is all about what you can do to keep up to date.

WHAT DO YOU NEED TO KEEP UP TO DATE WITH?

All these – in an ideal world:

- latest government legislation
- latest educational news
- latest news from your union
- developments in your specialist subject
- teaching strategies and latest research
- what interests 'kids of today'
- life, the universe and everything – after all, you are preparing the students to work in an ever-changing world!

HOW CAN YOU DO THIS?

Well, my advice would be to read up, but to choose the time to do this and select documents carefully. Of course, this will be entirely based on what type of teacher you are. One thing I learnt very quickly is that you cannot read everything, and the chances are you won't (see Paperwork, page 20). We are incredibly busy with our day-to-day working lives and on the vast majority of occasions, once at home, a teacher should relax and unwind.

The reality is though, that most teachers are marking, planning, writing reports, calculating statistics, creating resources and reading in their time away from the classroom. Below I list some ideas to help you keep up to date – maybe in ways that you may not have thought of – that you can incorporate into your commuting time, or simply ways to keep yourself up to date faster and smarter.

KEEP UP TO DATE

- **Talk to colleagues** I would wholeheartedly recommend that you visit other schools, observe colleagues and talk to colleagues as well. There is not enough time for colleagues to 'talk about teaching' in schools.

- **Read educational blogs and websites and get into tweeting** I love sharing ideas through blogs, emails and tweets, and saving articles to read. My online reading list is extensive. Save content that will stand the test of time to your favourites and read articles that are tailored for the current time of the academic year.

- **Tune in to government websites and sign up to subject-specific email alerts** This will inform you of the latest speeches, consultations and any new publications. You can then choose what to follow up.

- **Newspapers** Read educational articles in national papers and follow their education sections. Only you can work out what works best, whether this is every weekend or catching up on your subject-specific area during holidays. There is no rule other than this – keep up to speed with developments.

- **Podcasts** Not everyone has the time or inclination to sit down and read a newspaper or spend hours on the computer reading blogs. And for those with a long commute by car, educational podcasts can be an ideal way to keep up to date with all aspects of your job.

- **Books** There are so many fantastic books in publication – but pace yourself. As I look across to my reading shelf, I have about 30 educational books, most of them untouched and unread; others I have picked through and a small minority I have read cover to cover. I recommend you do dip in and out of your books as much as you can, even if you don't finish them. Treat them like ice-cream flavours – choose what you want.

- **Get to know the students** If you can properly get to know the students and find out what makes them tick, you can produce lessons that will inspire and prepare them for their futures (see page 92). Train yourself to meet their needs/wants.

- **Make the most of life outside the classroom** As well as this benefitting your own well-being (see page 40), your experiences outside the classroom will only help you inside the classroom: meeting people from other careers, you will learn more about the world of work your students may venture into; your hobbies and interests can provide inspiration for ways to teach particular topics in new and interesting ways…

- **CPD** (See page 110) Attend training courses. This is something you really should do! Some of the CPD can be formal, internally or externally within your school, or entirely informal and driven by you, such as attending a TeachMeet (see page 136) in the evening after school or on the weekend. If you're engaged online, you'll be very familiar with TeachMeets and will know that they can impact on your classroom practice in so many ways, compared to your bog-standard one-size-fits-all INSET day at school.

INNOVATION TIP

Keeping up to date is a mandatory aspect of your job as a teacher, but that is not the reason to do it. The reason to keep up to date is to keep your teaching and your subject alive to inspire and enthuse your students. If you teach a group of inquisitive 12-year-olds a topic in a way you loved five years ago, you will likely find what you taught then simply doesn't work today. Find new ways, new inspirations. You will enjoy it, and your students will too. Become Vitruvian, and keep evolving!

4
COLLABORATIVE

'As we drove past London's famous landmarks, teachers took the time to talk about classroom ideas – on the lower and upper decks – sharing work that had made an impact on their practice... It was magical!'

BE COLLABORATIVE

Throughout my career, I have relied on the support of my colleagues every single working day. It is impossible to work in a large secondary school with over 1,300 students and 200 staff without needing to offer or receive support.

DEVELOP A COLLABORATIVE FRAME OF MIND

Teamwork is vital, whether you are working with one other colleague, an entire department, a whole year team or on a project across the entire school. You may be able to work alone for a small period of time and show a degree of resilience, but you will have very little impact on students and colleagues over time if you do not develop a collaborative frame of mind from the outset.

COLLABORATIVE CAREER PROGRESSION

In your fourth year of teaching, the danger zone for attrition is closing in on you. It's important that you focus on what matters, ignore the nonsense, and work hand in hand with leadership teams to develop a stronger and more supportive school community, as well as considering your own well-being in and out of school.

For us all to become Vitruvian teachers, schools must give teachers the freedom to teach without fear of judgement, and the financial backing to engage with meaningful and long-term professional development. Schools that develop this culture are likely to have highly motivated teachers who will continue to work within the school, or only leave the school for promotion elsewhere, to relocate, or to work in other sectors of education.

By now, the formative years of your career have already been established. The genetic code of who you are as a teacher is in place. The template is now in place to create the teacher you want to be. The time has come to develop and embed your classroom practice, to enjoy and refine what you do before then going to take on a whole school responsibility of some kind. You are becoming Vitruvian.

It was in or around my sixth or seventh year of teaching, following leading my department through a successful subject Grim Reaper inspection, that I considered leaving my job in a successful school to try something different. I felt I had achieved all I could. However, in reality and with hindsight, I can see that I was nowhere near reaching my full potential! And neither was my department. Those teachers have all gone on to lead their own departments since, and like me still teach to this very day. We were a great department. We had real team spirit and supported each other through good times and bad times – through the highs and lows of everyday school life.

COLLABORATION AND BEING SUPPORTIVE

To be able to succeed long term in the teaching profession, you will need to develop a degree of resilience, aspiration and innovation with support from your colleagues. You will also need to master supporting others in a variety of contexts: coaching and mentoring newly qualified teachers; supporting staff on tailored CPD programmes; appraisal and performance management, as well as helping colleagues through difficult personal or professional times. To be successful in your own career, you will need to collaborate outside of your own classroom. No teacher I have ever known has made a good career out of teaching by working solo.

But don't forget that successful collaboration involves support from a much wider audience than just your colleagues. As you step up into taking on a whole school responsibility, you will need to engage with parents, governors and school visitors much more frequently. As you develop your experiences of working with others across the school community, your resilience will develop and you will need to toughen up. Hopefully you will start to see another aspect of school outside the four walls of your own classroom, and that another world of education co-exists in the very same working environment. It is a fascinating world where you begin to work with other professionals, consultants and colleagues in your own school.

WHAT IS COVERED IN THIS CHAPTER?

In this chapter you will discover what it means to work collaboratively with colleagues both within and outside your school, and the impact it can have on you as a professional.

- I discuss how you can go about creating and sharing your own classroom resources and using them further afield.

- I go on to explore the importance of collaborating with your peers, and address the difficulties of speaking in front of them.

- I explain how you can work with other adults in your classroom and how to organise your own professional development events, including working with other teachers in other schools to enhance your own and others' professional development.

- I discuss coaching other colleagues and placing yourself in situations that require you to be more thoughtful of others. For example, parents' evenings or leading school assemblies.

- And finally, I take a look at the wider picture – the collaborations with your local community outside of school, and with teachers from local schools and beyond.

I would not be the teacher I am today if I didn't share thoughts, resources and my time with others. After all, you will also demand the time – no matter how small the need – of your colleagues to support you throughout the many stages of your career .

SHARING RESOURCES

As teachers, we like to collaborate with each other within our own community and with colleagues in local schools, particularly when we need guidance, help and expertise from other colleagues. It's in our genetic make-up to share and care!

The concept and philosophy of sharing best practice will never die. And this is a good thing, because as teachers we should all share ideas with each other; working with tight budgets can make accessing new ideas to help students progress even more challenging. However, the landscape of teaching resources is changing because of social media. Today, I can share an idea online and receive instant feedback from colleagues within my own Professional Learning Network (PLN) of teachers who teach my subject, or those who have a general interest in the things I share online. This feedback can be far-reaching at times, sometimes from across the world – which is truly mind-blowing! I believe we can all achieve this.

But, what if other people took your ideas without consent or recognition? Or worse, took your beloved scheme of work and sold it on for a profit? How would you feel? These days, the issues surrounding copyright and teachers sharing resources freely are more complicated than ever. Social media has made the adaptation of ideas and resources as 'our own' even more achievable than before.

Blogs too have allowed teachers to keep memoirs and share their own thoughts and ideas of what is going on in their classrooms, or even within their school. In the past, we have become accustomed to – and restrained by – uploading resources into specific places in order to share, access and download information, but the online world is changing teaching practice and the sharing of resources

SHARING RESOURCES WITHIN YOUR DEPARTMENT AND WITH COLLEAGUES ACROSS YOUR SCHOOL

As I have said before, we should all share resources and ideas with each other. Within your department and your school, this should ideally be a team effort.

If resources are shared freely, it is common etiquette to ask and offer correct attribution to the owner, particularly if they are shared online!

Within your department, one person may be assigned the task of preparing the department or subject scheme of work. They may take it on themselves to create resources for you all to use. But the down side of one person creating resources is that the quality and content can be limited. It is much more beneficial to have a system in place whereby you and other colleagues in your department contribute to resources. If your head of department advises that each of you and your colleagues take turns to prepare resources for others and not just for yourself, then good on them. This is how it should be. It leads to a more collaborative culture!

WHAT WOULD YOU DO?
Tweet me @TeacherToolkit

A LONG TIME AGO, IN A LOCAL AUTHORITY FAR, FAR AWAY...

TEACHERS SHARED RESOURCES ON PAPER VIA THE NOTICEBOARD, THE BANDA MACHINE, BY POST AND GRADUALLY VIA THE PHOTOCOPYING MACHINE! TEACHERS WORKING TOGETHER WAS A MUCH MORE COLLABORATIVE AFFAIR. WITH THE ESTABLISHMENT OF SOCIAL MEDIA, TEACHERS MAY NOT REALISE THAT THEY ARE SHARING LESS AND LESS WITH THEIR OWN COLLEAGUES. THE OPPORTUNITY TO LOOK TO THE WORLD WIDE WEB IS TOO MUCH OF A DISTRACTION FROM LOOKING FOR EXPERTISE FROM WITHIN.

WHAT I WOULD ENCOURAGE TEACHERS TO DO, IS TO GET OFF THE COMPUTER AND GO AND LOOK AROUND THE OFFICES AND CLASSROOMS WITHIN THEIR OWN SCHOOL. SPEAK WITH COLLEAGUES AND SEEK ADVICE IN THE STAFFROOM. I'M CERTAIN YOU WILL DISCOVER A HIDDEN GEM – AN IDEA OR RESOURCE LYING RIGHT UNDER YOUR OWN NOSE!

DO NOT UNDERESTIMATE THE EXPERTISE THAT LIES WITHIN YOUR OWN SCHOOL. DO NOT FORGET THE IMPORTANCE OF SHARING IDEAS WITH COLLEAGUES THROUGH SIMPLE DISCUSSIONS, SHARING BEST PRACTICE OR SIMPLY GOING FOR A LITTLE 'NOSY' AROUND THE SCHOOL PREMISES IN SEARCH OF GOOD IDEAS.

SHARING RESOURCES WITH THE OUTSIDE WORLD BEYOND YOUR CLASSROOM

I think these days every teacher searches online for resources before looking anywhere else, even if it is right there in front of them. Teachers are sharing all sorts online:

- free resources
- paid for resources
- articles and books
- blogs about books we have read
- video snippets from lessons we have taught
- photos of example displays and images of students' work
- images of teaching, marking and student feedback.

The list is endless…

I MUST POINT OUT…

- No photos, videos or examples of students' work should be posted on websites or social media without the express permission of the school and, most importantly, the student or parent/carer.

- No resources should be posted on websites or social media for free or otherwise unless all contributors clearly permit this.

- If you created the resource yourself at your school, you should check your school contract before uploading it publicly.

There is very little awareness among teachers about intellectual property rights and ownership of teacher resources. Schools do very little to address this with their own staff. It may not be an issue, or it may be included in the small print within school–teacher contracts. Some teachers have clauses in their contract whereby the school retains the right to resources created in school time. **Check your employment contract** for clarification over this.

If you are unclear about what this all means for sharing your own resources online, the best thing to do is to bring it to the attention of your line manager. I have researched this issue for several years and the best source of information I can find which clarifies intellectual property for teachers is given below.

Toolkit essential: copyright rules

Let me be crystal-clear from the outset. If you are creating resources at home in your own time and not your school's, then as far as I understand it, these resources belong to you. Anything earnt or spent by you, is also your hard-earned cash! But if you create resources for your job role, and particularly during school time, these resources belong to the school. Read Copy Rights and Wrongs 'School & Copyright' (www.copyrights andwrongs.nen.gov.uk). It's vital reading!

DISCLAIMER: The information given here is for guidance only. I am not a legal expert. You must assure yourself of your legal rights.

PEER-TO-PEER PROFESSIONAL DEVELOPMENT

The key to collaboration is being able to work effectively with your peers for the benefit of your students, but also for the benefit of your own formative development, and to help others develop professionally too. Genuine and meaningful professional development can only happen when teachers are collaborating, and it is vital you do not lose the impetus for doing so. It is so easy for teachers to go it alone in schools; make sure you continue to share inside and outside your department and school.

This chapter builds on the ideas in the CPD chapter (see page 110) to focus even more on utilising our peers for our professional development. Every teacher, regardless of whether you are new to the profession, or an old hand like me, must be fully engaged in peer-to-peer professional development to become truly Vitruvian.

WHAT CONSTITUTES PEER-TO-PEER PROFESSIONAL DEVELOPMENT?

- **Simple conversations** Throughout your teaching career you will either inadvertently or deliberately seek the attention and feedback of your peers. In your first few years of teaching, this will happen frequently. In the best schools I have worked in, the classroom doors are always open. Of course, you will naturally turn towards colleagues who have become your friends, but my advice here would be to seek out a 'critical friend' – someone outside of your department or year group – a colleague who you trust but have a more professional relationship with, who can offer impartial critique when you most need it.

- **Lesson observations** How do you deal with your peers observing your practice? Recently, this was a fearful pastime for many teachers. But, the culture is now changing from one that stems from being judged in one-off observations, to one where the observation is part of an overall formative process of sustained support and review (see Observations, page 68 and CPD, page 110). This changing culture means that teachers can now listen carefully to feedback from a lesson observation rather than being sidetracked by the grade. The feedback can be more meaningful and observations can be tailored to the individual teacher.

- **Joint long-term project such as lesson study** Lesson study is a relatively new practice in the UK, but has been around for over a century in Japan. It is a specific method of lesson observation where teachers work in small groups (usually threes) to plan, carry out and review observations, where the focus is on what an agreed group of students learn/achieve/take from the observation rather than on what the teacher does or doesn't do. (See Bibliography.)

- **TeachMeets** Informal conferences such as TeachMeets (for example, researchEd, TMLondon, SLTeachMeet and Northern Rocks) are a relatively new grassroots teacher-training revolution. They are typically organised by teachers for teachers, usually through social media, and held at various school and university venues all over the UK. Most events are listed on this single website: This type of powerful professional development welcomes all teachers to the platform to share what they are doing in their

classrooms. It is transformational for those attending, and even more so for teachers brave enough to step up and present in front of their peers. It is all about bringing colleagues together to share best practice out of a conference setting and hear what other teachers have to share. In my opinion, this is far better than a conference organised by a company that requires a school to pay out over £300 to send one teacher on a one-day event in a local hotel, with the only takeaway being a memorable lunch! TeachMeets are exciting CPD that has impact in the classroom the very next day!

- **In-school TeachMeets** This is exactly as it sounds: a TeachMeet-style CPD event for staff working within a single school – with no external visitors in attendance. It is organised and hosted within the allocated training days or a twilight session. It is **all** staff attending and sharing in front of their

peers. In my experience, teachers are reluctant to speak or present in front of colleagues within their own school. The idea is that in-school TeachMeets are more informal than a standard CPD day, and that this informality will help reduce teachers' fear of talking in front of their colleagues – something that can only be of benefit to an ethos of collaboration within the school. This CPD is the kind of teacher-training and resource-sharing that needs to start happening in schools during the working day, not just after school guided hours! I want to make in-school TeachMeets a frequent occurrence and a model for all.

I no doubt will come across as a huge fan of the TeachMeets. **However**, I do need to say that even though we can and should all do this, it should also be balanced against our own priorities and the needs of individual teachers.

'IF THERE IS A SINGLE THING I WOULD RECOMMEND ALL TEACHERS TO DO, IT WOULD BE TO ATTEND A LOCAL TEACHMEET, ORGANISED BY TEACHERS, FOR TEACHERS.'

@TeacherToolkit

Work, and more specifically CPD, **cannot always be engaging**. To significantly develop sometimes requires hard work and, sometimes, hard work – or at least long-term professional development – is not fun. Alternatively, you could just keep on attending TeachMeets over a long period of time, and heighten your CPD experiences…

My London bus TeachMeet

There are, of course, many variations on the TeachMeet model. I know, because I once organised a TeachMeet event on a London bus for 50 passengers (teachers)! As we drove around London's famous landmarks, teachers took the time to talk about classroom ideas – on the lower and upper decks – sharing work that had made an impact on their practice and on their own students in their classrooms. It was magical!

TOP TIPS FOR COLLABORATIVE
PEER-TO-PEER PROFESSIONAL DEVELOPMENT

Teacher's fear: **Peer-to-peer solution:**

An observer talking about the teacher's lesson behind their back to other teachers.

▶ A school professional development code of conduct that stipulates confidentiality and that feedback is for the teacher being observed only.

It is more nerve-wracking presenting in front of your peers – you have to see them again the next day, which can make you feel awkward!

▶ Remember, we are all teachers; we are all working in the same school – albeit it at different stages of our careers – and the chances are we are all feeling the same! It is only awkward if you allow it to be...

It's embarrassing sharing in front of your peers.

▶ Nothing ventured, nothing gained. If you don't share, you will never know if anyone else feels the same way. Some you win, some you lose!

Standing up and speaking at an INSET day in your school.

▶ It's not for everyone, but it's incredibly empowering. Try meeting in the middle and presenting in small groups in a classroom carousel model to allow your confidence to grow.

Standing up and speaking at another external event.

▶ You may or may not feel comfortable doing this at first until you have practised speaking with colleagues in your own school. For me, I felt more confident speaking to colleagues I didn't know before developing the ability to speak in front of my peers. Find out which method works for you.

Sharing your resources with the world.

▶ Start small. Share your resources with colleagues, then with others in nearby schools. If the feedback is positive, upload your resources on to a website or a blog and share them with the world.

PLAN YOUR OWN TEACHMEET

This is my simple guide to organising your own TeachMeet event; the best type of CPD currently available for all teachers and educators across the UK! (See the previous two pages for more information on TeachMeets.)

My first piece of advice is to make sure that you attend a TeachMeet before planning your own! While you are there, research all aspects of the event, from the catering to the ticketing, the hosting and how to curate a programme with a range of guest presenters who will all arrive at one place, on time and speak for free.

YOUR FULL GUIDE TO PLANNING A TEACHMEET

CHECKLIST FOR SCHOOLS PLANNING A TEACHMEET

Your school will need to have/be able to provide the following:

- ☐ The backing and agreement of your senior leadership team, as well as willing and excited attendees. You will need two or three other colleagues to lend a hand.

- ☐ Site staff on hand and available until the end, and perhaps some student helpers at the beginning to hand out leaflets and give directions.

- ☐ An open reception/welcome/map of the school and name badges printed off for people when they arrive.

- ☐ Catering staff, facilities and yummy refreshments!

- ☐ A warm and comfortable venue that can hold 100–200 people seated.

- ☐ ICT facilities (see *Toolkit essential: TeachMeet ICT* on the next page).

- ☐ A host to open the event with a welcome (ideally the CPD leader or headteacher).

- ☐ Clean toilets and car parking.

- ☐ A holding website for ticketing and a Twitter profile to promote the event.

- ☐ School contact details, directions, information about the event (for example, times and a list of guest speakers) and information about the local area (places to eat and stay).

CHECKLIST FOR A TEACHER PLANNING A TEACHMEET

As a teacher organiser you will need to:

☐ Advertise the event via posters in school, a holding website and social media.

☐ Organise a compère and some co-hosts to help lead the event.

☐ Update information on blogs and TeachMeet websites; get everyone promoting!

☐ Organise the tickets using Eventbrite (www.eventbrite.co.uk). Lead-in time should typically be two to three months minimum. Tickets generally sell out within four weeks and at least 10% will drop out as the event is free. It's a good idea to have a reserve list in case of drop-outs.

☐ Collate speakers and biographies for the event. Seek a keynote speaker if you want to raise the profile.

☐ Seek ethical sponsorship and free prizes (see opposite).

☐ Prepare the venue for arrival, and expect to be last to leave as you clear up!

☐ Meet and greet everyone, and close the evening with thanks and goodbyes.

☐ Gather an incredible amount of expertise, excitement and collaboration in one room.

☐ Set the mood for the event; encourage a light-hearted atmosphere, full of risk and freedom. Win-win!

Toolkit essential: TeachMeet ICT

- **Wifi network to support 100+ users** so that attendees are able to use their portable devices to log in to a wifi network with a simple domain name and password. The wifi should have the capacity to support 100+ users. This will allow those inside and out to follow the conversation – called a backchannel – with a dedicated Twitter hashtag for the event, for example, #TMLondon.

- **Main screen** to display: a) holding slide/video on arrival plus guest presentations; b) to be able to go between presentations and Name Picker Tool which is used to select the presenters at random.

- **Second screen** to display a live Twitter feed to the audience, large enough to be able to be read from the back of the room. A suitable application is Twitterfall or TweetBeam.

- **Sound** for presentations and video as well as a microphone (ideally hands-free) for presenters to use. [Note: if using a hands-free microphone, check that the batteries are fully charged!]

- **Connectivity for different hardware** for example for iMacs, iPads and other devices.

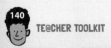

WHAT YOU WILL GET OUT OF IT

- 100+ enthusiastic attendees visiting your school. What kudos!

- Plenty of press opportunities to raise your reputation among your local schools, and forge links with others.

- Free CPD for all your staff, should you encourage them to come. It is incredibly rare for attendees to leave with no new ideas, contacts, insights or further opportunities.

- The warm glow of feeling that you have contributed to an incredibly powerful and growing epidemic.

- A skip in your step for weeks…

TOP TIPS FOR SPONSORSHIP AND PRIZES

In return for sponsorship or prizes, offer to include a company logo on publicity material. You could include a brief statement to recognise their contribution, and pass on any special offers to attendees.

Offer to feature the company name in all promotion about the event. The sponsorship donation will been seen by thousands of people through social media; at least 100 people during the TeachMeet evening itself; plus those that tune in online via audio and video feed. Predict the number of people that could be exposed to the event via social media; count up the follower reach and use this to entice potential sponsors.

Try to get people to:

- sponsor the refreshments

- sponsor a conference pack, or leaflets to go in the pack

- sponsor the production and printing of certificates for the evening (to include their logo)

- donate a prize: gift vouchers, a subscription, a camera, a tablet

- sponsor live audio or video content on the web.

Turn over to find the 5 minute TeachMeet plan!

5 MINUTE TEACHMEET PLAN

... photocopy or download, and scribble your way to an inspiring and informal CPD session for teachers!

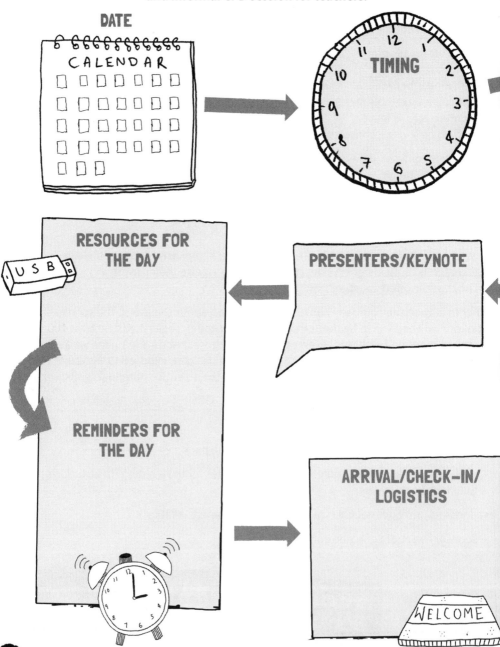

DATE

CALENDAR

TIMING

RESOURCES FOR THE DAY

USB

PRESENTERS/KEYNOTE

REMINDERS FOR THE DAY

ARRIVAL/CHECK-IN/ LOGISTICS

WELCOME

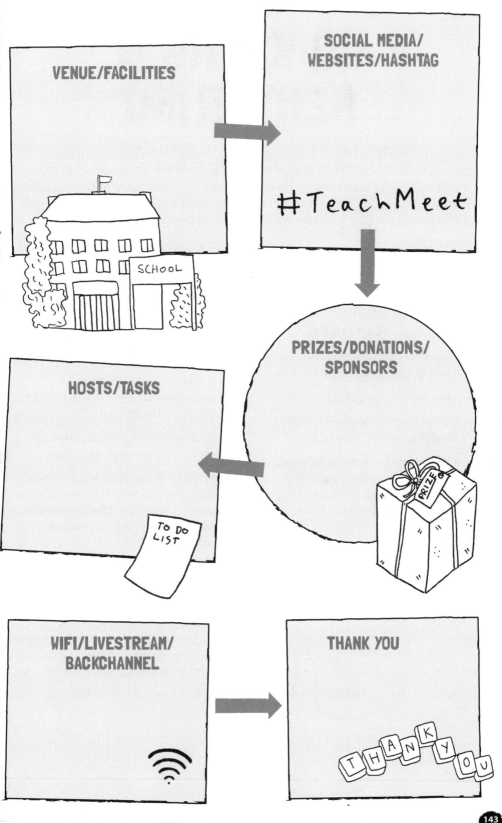

VENUE/FACILITIES

SOCIAL MEDIA/
WEBSITES/HASHTAG

#TeachMeet

PRIZES/DONATIONS/
SPONSORS

HOSTS/TASKS

TO DO
LIST

PRIZE

WIFI/LIVESTREAM/
BACKCHANNEL

THANK YOU

THANK YOU

COACHING & MENTORING

There is no greater privilege than being in a position to coach or mentor another colleague. The chances are that after receiving your fair share of coaching and mentoring in your earlier years, you will soon have the opportunity to do this yourself. This may be coaching the next cohort of NQTs, or coaching another member of staff who is new to the school, or with a specific focus to help improve their teaching.

COACHING

Coaching can be used by a variety of people in a variety of situations:

- a recently qualified teacher working with a newly qualified teacher
- a head of department working with a recently qualified teacher
- a teacher coaching another teacher
- a member of the leadership team coaching a head of department
- a specialist such as a psychologist, counsellor, or an assessor such as a dyslexia specialist, working with a teacher to a set brief.

Context:

- planning and/or observing lessons
- providing lesson feedback
- reviewing projects, resources, lessons.

MENTORING

Mentoring can be used by a variety of people in a range of situations:

- a teacher needing job application help
- a teacher asking for advice concerning a group of students
- a teacher working with an occupational health officer to build up their confidence
- an inexperienced headteacher asking for advice from their governors.

Mentoring is essential for your career development, and I would advise every teacher to surround themselves with colleagues from all education sectors. Keep your critical friends in your pocket and consider very honest and transparent 360-degree reviews where you assess your own knowledge and skills, but seek the opinions of four or five other colleagues to provide you with the feedback you need. You may work with a coach in order to address the feedback you have received from your mentors.

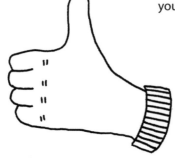

WORKING WITH YOUR TA

I've worked with many teaching assistants (TAs) over the years, and the most important piece of advice that I can give, is this:

Teachers need time to talk with their teaching assistants to plan lessons and discuss student needs.

This can be difficult. In many of the secondary schools I have worked in, I have rarely been aware of who is attending my class because the needs of the child change so frequently. It can be very difficult for any SENCO to balance the needs of the students, versus the needs of teaching assistants and the teachers.

'Teachers must deploy support staff effectively.' (DfE Teachers' Standards)

At all costs, the student is the number one priority.

It is our duty as teachers to direct TAs in our class, even if we have had no time to plan collaboratively, or did not expect them to arrive there! After all, the TA is there to support the child, and you need to do all you can to facilitate this.

Can you imagine following one child from subject to subject across an entire secondary school? And being able to support possibly five different teachers throughout the day in a range of specialist subjects, and potentially up to GCSE standard? I know I'd struggle. TAs are given very little professional development to cope with this demand, and yet they need to be able to grasp what is going on in your lesson immediately and to think on their feet to be able to help the students they are supporting. They have a demanding role, and need your support and advice.

Letter to ex-Secretary of State Mr Michael Gove regarding teaching assistants, by Cherryl Drabble

In her letter, Drabble speaks out to the former Education Secretary about proposed cuts to the number of teaching assistants. Her letter is poignant, noble and definitely worth reading. Here are just some of her points:

- 'They are the most valuable resource I have.'
- 'We plan all of our activities together so that everyone has ownership of the plans and can see the bigger picture and what we are trying to achieve.'
- 'Each TA has been specially trained for a certain role according to their talents and interests.'
- '[They] can make lessons accessible for my children like no one I've ever seen.'
- 'As I'm a senior leader, I'm often taken out of class for various reasons. Guess who steps in as teacher during my absence?'

cherrylkd.wordpress.com/2013/06/08/letter-to-mr-gove-re-teaching-assistants-please-rt/

USE YOUR TA!

'Teachers must develop effective professional relationships with colleagues, knowing how and when to draw on advice and specialist support.'
(DfE Teachers' Standards.)

For the hundreds of colleagues that I have worked with, one of the most frequent sticking points has been the ability to adapt teaching (live in the lesson) to respond to the strengths and needs of all students – knowing when and how to differentiate appropriately, by having an awareness of their physical, social and intellectual needs. Cue: use your TA!

The Education Endowment Foundation recently published a guidance document for teachers and school leaders entitled 'Making Best Use of Teaching Assistants' that said:

'Recent research demonstrates that when [teaching assistants] are well trained and used in structured settings with high-quality support and training, teaching assistants can make a noticeable positive impact on pupil learning.'

The findings publish seven **evidence-based recommendations** to help schools make better use of teaching assistants, split into three areas:

- 'recommendations on the use of teaching assistants in everyday classroom contexts'

- 'recommendations on the use of teaching assistants in delivering structured interventions out of class'

- 'recommendations on linking learning from work led by teachers and TAs'.

Read the full report here!

COLLABORATION TIP

- Give your TA copies of resources to take away for their own preparation.
- Share with them the context of a particular lesson in advance.
- Find out about their talents – perhaps speaking a second language, having qualifications in counselling or psychology, having previously worked in another profession – and utilise them in your lessons.
- Give your TA an opportunity to teach part of the lesson.

Toolkit essential: working with TAs

1. Provide TAs with support at the right time, and help them prioritise tasks. If they are attached to you in a primary setting, this will be much easier to do as the likelihood is that they are attached to a year group/class teacher. In a secondary school, this is much more unlikely. Help your TA to prioritise the support they offer by providing them with a list of important and not-so-important things to help support the class.

2. Help TAs grasp subject terminology – in advance – before they are put in a position where they have to extrapolate definitions and meaning in the lesson for students.

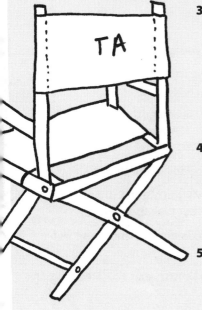

3. Encourage TAs to take a step back and help develop students' resilience and independence. Of course, an individual context will be needed here. This may mean taking a step back from questioning and offering 'reflection time' for students, rather than helping with the answer immediately…

4. When TAs use questioning with students, avoid closed questions such as 'Who is?' and 'What did?' to develop more open-ended questioning that leads to further complex demands. For example, 'Why will?' or 'How might?'

5. Ask the TA to avoid repeating what you have instructed the class to do. Encourage the TA to insist that the student listens to the teacher in the first instance and avoids 'spoon-feeding'.

PARENTS' EVENINGS

You should always be fully prepared for every parents' evening. And of course, when I state 'parents', this can be defined as parents and carers, uncles, aunties and cousins… Believe me, every possible person will attempt to represent a student at 'parents' evening'.

RULE ONE: Never be late. Yes you. The teacher!
RULE TWO: Dress smartly if that is the expectation of the school.
RULE THREE: Know every single student by name, and know them well!
RULE FOUR: Smile, listen and look to build or strengthen a relationship.
RULE FIVE: End the conversation with a key message to take away.

I've always been very good at keeping with rules one and two, but number three is the one I have struggled with. Why? Well, because the very nature of my own specialist subject restricts me from knowing every single student. Projects are limited to between 8 and12 weeks' curriculum time as students rotate on a design technology carousel. This is quite different from teaching a child in your subject for the entire academic year, as in other subjects. However, as a result I do believe it has put me in a very good position to be able to impart advice on knowing students well for parents evening. I would argue that we technology teachers are some of the best-equipped teachers in secondary schools for developing survival strategies for dealing with parents' evenings. In this chapter, I will offer you own my parents' evening survival strategies.

PARENTS' EVENING TOP SURVIVAL STRATEGIES

1. PREPARE BEFOREHAND

- Know every student in your class. Have one thing you can say about them.

- Have a short action plan prepared for each student. This could be a simple bullet point as an aide-memoire.

- Prepare a simple crib sheet (see opposite) with key headings that you must discuss. (Note: for the most difficult students – if I see them – I **always** ask the family for a mobile number and email address. Always!)

- Plan for a short period of time for the parent or carer to ask questions.

- Plan to also include some time for the student to ask you questions. If they don't, have some key 'closed' questions planned to tease out their thoughts.

- If you have student photos, books or exemplar documents to hand, these will always help you.

- Lay a watch or a clock on your table to ensure you keep to your allocated time. This also offers a subliminal cue that time is precious.

- Take a bottle of water and a throat lozenge. Coffee or tea may help temporarily, but water is essential for that happy teacher's voice.

Student: _____

Attendance and punctuality at lessons:

_____

Preparation for lessons, e.g. equipment, books and homework:

_____

Focus in class, e.g. attitude, participation, teamwork and individual effort:

_____

Behaviour:

_____

General class work:

_____

Formative/Summative assessments:

_____

Parting comments/takeaway:

_____

Contact details if wanted/needed:

_____

Discussion notes:

_____

_____

_____

Action plan:

_____

_____

_____

2. GET OFF TO A GOOD START

I know it's almost absurd to offer such advice, but basic human principles apply here, no matter whom you are talking to and no matter what the context of the conversation. When you greet a parent or carer, stand up from your table and chair, smile and offer a handshake. It makes a real difference, even when dealing with the most difficult parents or carers and/or conversations. Take into account cultural preferences; for example, it may be that no handshake is required.

3. HAVE A BACK-UP PLAN

If you get off to a bad start, turn the tables and ask the parents what they would like to know. Offer a range of suggestions – after all, you are the expert – and allow the parents or carers to select what information they would like to receive. You can still add in the information that you would like to communicate under the umbrella of 'behaviour' or 'progress', or whatever else is suitable in that given situation. Parents want to know what they can do to support their child. It is your duty to open the door…

4. KNOW HOW TO TALK TO PARENTS OR CARERS OF REALLY BADLY BEHAVED STUDENTS

In this situation, I always direct the conversation to the student only. I insist that parents and carers are **not** allowed to speak. It takes a great deal of confidence to be able to do this – and sustain it throughout – but it works if you can guide the conversation so that the student finds their own solutions sitting alongside their family. You will be surprised how many parents actually follow the request not to speak in a heart-to-heart. Ask particular types of closed questions to dictate and direct the conversation towards a possible action plan. It's a winning strategy!

Ultimately, you want your message to be heard and received. You want parental support, and for this message to be clear and succinct. During this conversation, if you can find – even with the hardest to reach student – a middle ground to help them feel that they are not necessarily being told off, or being made to feel inadequate, then you are already making progress.

5. KEEP THE CONVERSATION ON TRACK

At times the conversation may veer away from what you want to say, either towards what the parents or carers 'want you to say', or 'what they want to hear'. It takes a great deal of confidence to set the record straight – particularly in your first few years of teaching – and to do this with precision and aplomb. For the most difficult students, have something succinct planned and be prepared to disagree in the most contentious situation. It's the difficult conversations that you haven't planned for that you need to equip yourself for the most. Keep to the point, and do not deviate!

In these situations, stay calm and refer back to your crib sheet. Focus on the key point and keep it simple. Don't fuel the conversation or ask leading questions, and if questioned, always retort with your key sentence/feedback. It may be difficult, but you will feel better knowing that you have remained professional and dealt with the situation calmly.

6. BRING THE MEETING TO A CLOSE

If you have set your stop watch to the prescribed time beforehand, this will be a formality. If not, there are two non-verbal cues you can rely on to bring any positive/ negative conversation to an end. They are: a) at the end of your sentence summary, stand up and offer a handshake to say your goodbyes, or b) use the long queue of parents behind you as a 'cue' to end proceedings. Use the former if no other parents are waiting, or you need the conversation to come to an end...

Role play time

Scenario 1: A parent and student come to meet you, you stand up and shake hands but you have forgotten the child's name!

Quick fix 1 Use your teacher planner, registers or data-tracking sheets to your advantage.

> *'Hi, take a seat. If you can just locate your 'surname' here on this list while I [peer over the book and] find your data/book/homework.'*

While you find the document (or example) you can look to see where the student is pointing in your teacher planner.

Quick fix 2 Have an up-to-date seating plan to hand. It's a great visual cue if you do have a momentary lapse of concentration. If the plan includes student photographs, even easier!

Scenario 2: It is clear that there has been a kerfuffle between the parent and child prior to coming to see you. Your comments could make a volatile situation worse.

Quick fix 1 This student has been doing well in your lessons so you can deliver meaningful praise and help ease the tension between them. This often results in the student warming to you and your subject.

Quick fix 2 You had issues you wanted to discuss with this child. You make the professional decision to end the appointment earlier than expected and explain that you will give the parents a phone call within the week.

Scenario 3: A translator is needed.

Quick fix 1 You trust the student to communicate key messages both ways and accurately. All you then need to do, is to draw on your observational skills to interpret facial expressions and voice intonation, with the added thumbs up or down for good measure.

Quick fix 2 It is clear that the messages are not getting through and the conversation becomes very short and succinct. This is particularly heart breaking when you would like to provide good news; explicit feedback; wish to give the student a good telling-off and make the parent 100% aware of it. Arrange a later appointment and ask the school to hire an interpreter.

BEST PRACTICE

1. If there is a language barrier, have a translator lined up.

2. An agreement between all three parties: the child; you and the family.

3. A strong message for improvement sandwiched between a positive introduction and conclusion.

4. A bottle of water to help keep you hydrated.

5. Examples of work available to share with the student and their parent or carer.

WORST PRACTICE

1. A teacher hiding behind a laptop or pile of marking!

2. A teacher not confident about their subject, the child or their progress.

3. A parent dictating the process.

4. A parent using the information to berate their child and devalue the conversation.

5. A student unable to engage with the conversation through no fault of their own, for example: the entire family being there as a distraction, or a two-year-old sibling dictating proceedings!

COLLABORATION TIP

Ask the student to place themselves upon the scale, indicating their overall performance to date.

This simple action can reveal so much about a child, for example their confidence, their self-belief… Take the role of coach and aim to encourage students to talk openly. Insist that parents play a listening role and that the focus of the conversation is specific and explicit. Aim to use this conversation to develop a fully collaborative action plan between you, the student and their family.

1. Consider overall performance to date; attendance, behaviour, effort.

2. Ask the student to mark their personal assumption on the scale.

3. Use the number as an indicator of their performance. It will also inform you about their self-perception. Ask them to set verbal targets with you in order to work towards being higher up the scale.

4. Set two or three targets and keep priorities succinct.

5. Take a photo of the scale at the end of the parents' evening and share it with students in their next lesson.

LEADING ASSEMBLIES

The school assembly delivers the whole school vision and sets the ethos for the day, the week and the term.

To make assemblies work, and make them work well, involves collaboration. In advance of the day it will involve preparation with other staff and students. On the day itself, it is highly possible that those presenting will involve more than just you! Be prepared to collaborate on content, style and delivery…

I love leading school assemblies now. But rewind to the start of my teaching career and you would never have caught me doing it. Until, that is, one day when it was landed on me. I was a new and still very young middle leader working in a brand-new school. There was nobody to speak on behalf of the faculty but me!

Many teachers crumble and their legs turn to jelly when faced with public speaking to any audience over 18 years old, or over 20 people in a room. But don't worry; not everyone needs to lead an assembly. That said, you are still likely to have to speak in an assembly to give a quick announcement as a form tutor, as a representative of your subject or to share student successes at some point or another. So, be prepared!

THE BEST ASSEMBLIES

- communicate one clear meaning
- are well delivered – consider rehearsing in front of a mirror!
- have clearly been well prepared, rehearsed and timed
- are student-led or involve students
- are meaningful and avoid endless notices
- feature the art of storytelling and create opportunities for laughter
- share best practice and celebrate student success
- give whole school messages to reinforce the ethos
- reinforce discipline
- include outside guests that capture the imagination and make learning real.

THE WORST ASSEMBLIES

- overrun
- are not well delivered; for example, the presenter cannot be heard at the back
- bore the students who start to fidget
- are delivered in an uncomfortable setting
- require ICT equipment that doesn't work; there is no plan B; the presenter wastes time trying to get it to work
- are full of messages and minutes
- finish far too early, requiring someone to step in and ad lib
- focus on student behaviour and spend too long telling the students off
- try to address difficult issues, for example, drugs or sex, without the wise intervention of outside specialists.

Toolkit essential: leading an assembly

1. **Consider your audience and the context of the assembly** Think about which Key Stage or age group it is for, the time of year and any other relevance the assembly needs to have.

2. **What are the objectives?** All good assemblies – aside from the necessary announcements – should have an objective. Make it purposeful for everyone in the room.

3. **Are there any real-life references that can be used?** What is happening in the media? I have often used the morning news, for example, for an assembly that same day. Make sure that any real-life references are relevant to the age group.

4. **What do you want to stick in the minds of your students?** Assemblies are much more than just a moment for collective worship or reflection; they are an opportunity for learning beyond the classroom. Like all good lessons, assemblies should be planned carefully to identify the learning outcomes. What is the fundamental aspect of the assembly you need students to grasp? What understanding should students take away? If any teachers were to speak with students after the assembly, what should students continue to know/understand?

5. **The best assemblies involve a range of students** At what point – if applicable – will you involve the audience? Will there be demonstrations requiring participation, or some basic questioning during the assembly? What about leading up to the presentation? Many teachers involve students days before the assembly by getting them to prepare presentations.

6. **Rehearse, rehearse, rehearse!** Practise timings and make sure you have prepared a plan A and a plan B. It's almost guaranteed that something will not go according to plan. What if ICT resources are unavailable on the day, your video presentation doesn't work or a student you need to contribute is absent? You must always be prepared for this. In most schools I have worked in, a planned assembly must always go ahead.

7. **Plan less rather than more** Assemblies have a tendency to overrun. I've rarely given an assembly and been able to deliver all the information I want to share in line with the timings I had originally planned. Have some additional information to share if needed – something not vital to your assembly theme and message, but something that is in keeping with your presentation. That said, I refer back to the previous point: rehearse and pick out the key information that must be shared – timing is everything!

8. **What reflective moments are needed?** I've worked in two faith schools. Even if you yourself are not practising the faith identified by the school, you may be expected to offer a moment for reflection. This could be a simple prayer, a poem or a still contemplation.

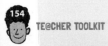

9. **How will students enter or exit the venue?** Is this something you will need to lead? Will there be music or videos on arrival/exit to reinforce the message or mood? Do you need to provide the means to do this, or is this already planned into the assembly programme?

10. **Consider your ICT requirements** Sound, visual and audio. Have a back-up plan just in case the video, USB or ICT resources do not work. There may be a power cut that morning!

11. **What other resources will you need?** Do you have any visual cue cards to hold up, or other props? Make sure you have prepared these well in advance. Don't rely on the photocopier being free 5 minutes before the assembly is due to start!

12. **Remember to use the assembly to reinforce the positive school values and ethos** Celebrate achievements, and utilise this time to offer praise and recognition for students in the community. Save the 'targeted' telling-off for smaller rooms with four (smaller) walls and fewer ears.

GETTING THE MOST OUT OF GOING TO ASSEMBLIES

As a teacher you will sit (or most likely stand) through hundreds of assemblies. You will be able to reel off the best and the worst assemblies at the drop of a hat. My advice to you is to use this time to properly learn from your colleagues; recall the times when you find you have been totally absorbed (or not) by an assembly, remembering all the reasons and values that brought you into teaching in the first place. Do you leave the school hall with a spring in your step knowing that the school is a better place? You should!

Ask yourself the following:

- What was so great about a particular assembly?

- What was it about the way the presenter delivered the assembly that made it work so well?

- What could I take from it to try in my next assembly?

And for those assemblies that leave you banging your head against the wall, then consider:

- What went wrong?

- What made you so frustrated?

Turn every assembly into a learning opportunity for yourself. Take note of what works and what doesn't, and re-use 'what works' whenever you have to speak in front of a group of students/staff at school, assembly or other events.

   'Oh, it's your assembly! I'm so glad it's not (so and so)…'

COLLABORATION TIP

While it might seem as if you are left to your own devices to prepare and deliver your own assembly, it's important to realise how much collaboration is really required. You will need to speak with the pastoral lead of the students involved, the site-team to plan the organisation of furniture, as well as the ICT support staff who will help you set up the presentation requirements. Do all this well before you have even spoken to your students and colleagues about the content and delivery of your assembly. Collaboration is key!

Remember, your assembly will set the tone for the day. How the students leave your assembly can impact on the lessons that follow. After an engaging assembly, they feel satisfied and ready to learn. After a long, boring assembly they will be restless and slow to concentrate. Students will most likely forget your key message and return to class unsettled and unfocused.

For the sake of colleagues as well as the students, it is important for all teachers to do their very best to plan, rehearse and deliver engaging assemblies. This is paramount for reinforcing the ethos and expectations of the school.

Do not plan any assembly in isolation. Involve your students and colleagues.

LOCAL SCHOOLS & THE WIDER COMMUNITY

As a young teacher, I didn't think about much beyond my classroom. All I could do was concentrate on my marking, planning and teaching. I hardly got out of my own department, let alone took the time to explore the local area. You'd be surprised how many of the experienced colleagues you work with still haven't explored any further than their classroom or department!

Today, as a school CPD leader, I believe it is essential to have CPD sessions dotted around the entire school (see the CPD chapter, page 110). This ensures that colleagues visit each other's classrooms, see displays and experience best practice in other pockets of the school. I believe that this should reach further than within the school. You only have to look at my web page www.TeacherToolkit.me to see how important social media is to me as a way for all teachers to share ideas and collaborate with others, no matter where they are geographically.

Your school's local community is a very special place – after all, it is where your students live! As you grow with experience (and age) you will appreciate how demographics, politics, finance, housing, social mobility, race, age and gender all have an impact on your local community and ultimately your school. These factors can dictate your school admissions, your school funding agreements and the natural evolution of your school, and schools nearby.

It is essential for schools to work hard to forge links with their local communities and other schools. This chapter aims to give you just a few ideas to get you started.

Twitter name? @schooltruth
Name in real life? Fiona Miller
What's her job? Journalist and school govenrnor
Specialist topic? Campaigning for better schools and a better education system
Why should I follow her? Miller used to work for the Blairs in Downing Street after the 1997 election. She co-founded the Local Schools Network and is active in national schools policy. She believes we can 'improve and achieve excellent public services while keeping them inclusive, firmly rooted in the local community and accountable to the people they serve.'

Toolkit essential: getting involved in your local community

- Attend local fairs, festivals and carnivals.

- Spend an evening or weekend simply exploring the local area. I cannot emphasise this enough!

- Your school may have sports facilities used by clubs and perhaps local community classes in the evening for ICT, arts, drama, sport, languages and so forth. Why not find something that you are interested in and go along? Zumba, badminton, karate… You name it, I've seen it all going on in my school after school hours. It's a great way to get to know members of the local community.

- Attend your school PTA (Parent Teacher Association) and quiz nights.

- Make sure you volunteer to help at the school summer fair.

- Volunteer to go on duty at lunchtime. If, like one of the schools I've worked in, your school is right on the doorstep of the local high street, surrounded by shops, cafés and businesses, then head out there at lunchtime. A teacher presence can help maintain a safe environment for students near a busy high road; it also ensures a public school presence for shopkeepers. I really enjoyed these kinds of duties. I've never before chatted to so many members of the public about our students – there was time for the odd 10-second window shopping too, and some welcome headspace!

Schools work best when they work in partnership w

Toolkit essential: collaborating with other local schools

- Invite colleagues from another local school into your school/classroom to share a common interest. This can be something as simple as a football match between schools or a local social event such as a TeachMeet or networking event.

- Invite colleagues from another local school into yours to share best practice. This could be a departmental forum for exchanging ideas within the local authority. This is also a great opportunity to bring like-minded teachers together to share the highs and lows of your subject expertise.

- Visit other local schools yourself to share their best practice. I would strongly recommend that every teacher gets out of their own school at least once a year!

- Set up links for coaching and mentoring across local schools. This can be achieved through the use of Lesson Study (see page 135) and IRIS Connect lesson observation (see page 75).

- Get involved with joint ventures and longer-term projects, such as mass choir events between schools, or curriculum projects that require utilising each others' resources and facilities.

- Have a critical friend at another local school. Swap emails and share thoughts regularly. Aim to meet once a term…

- Volunteer to get involved with your school teams in all local inter-school competitions, whether they be sports, arts, chess or public speaking. This is a great way to see other schools and meet the teachers and members of the local community.

other and with their local and wider communities.

A FINAL WORD ON COLLABORATION...

Collaborative colleagues share and work with others to develop themselves and each other as teachers and raise standards in schools. These colleagues need to be active in our own schools and should also be within reach of our local communities, but it doesn't need to stop there. Our local collaborative communities need not be teachers; use expertise in other sectors of business to support the work you do for students.

I have, at the click of a button, hundreds of colleagues dotted all over the world who I can turn to for absolutely anything: job application advice; proofreading my CV; advice on dealing with some very difficult and delicate situations; general feedback on school documentation or, more often than not, some random idea that I've dreamt up at 3 o'clock in the morning! And trust me, from the hundreds of people on social media in these teacher communities, there will be someone, somewhere in the world, ready to reply! Collaborative colleagues may even be on your doorstep and may offer to come and see you when required.

If you cannot get this sort of collaboration in your own school when the school gates are closed, social media and established networks around the community offer you a reliable alternative. Welcome to Vitruvian teaching!

5
ASPIRATIONAL

'I am aspirational. I am resilient. Despite the bombardment, political interference and the experience of redundancy, I am still here working with students and colleagues year in, year out.'

BE ASPIRATIONAL

My wife always tells me that success is what you make it. She is right. Teaching is a brilliant career. It is hard, but it is utterly rewarding. Of course I know nothing else, but I also know that I am in the right job for myself and the students I work with.

ASPIRATION IN A CHANGING WORLD

To be working as a teacher in your fifth year or more, is a small cause for celebration in today's climate. I entered teaching thinking that I would be doing this for life. So far, so good! I saw it as a vocation, but I'm not sure other people do. A reason for this may be that the world has changed since I first entered the profession in the early 1990s; the introduction of the world wide web and the social media epoch has made the world a smaller place to live in. We have many more opportunities to see the world than ever before; to connect with like-minded people, schools and classrooms all over the globe! This has, of course, changed our mindset and our view of what we can achieve. It may also have changed our aspirations…

As an18-year-old, entering into university to start a teacher training degree, I knew I was walking into a career that I would be happy doing for the rest of my life. However, 20 years in, I'm feeling battle-weary and I look into the distance, having not yet reached the halfway mark towards retirement and unsure of what teaching will constitute 20 years from now! Not that I am discontented with what I am doing at present or fearful of change. I say this with reference to what lies ahead with regard to the current workload placed upon teachers.

Teaching has always been demanding and exhausting. The focus on data, rising expectations and schools following business models have all changed the culture of the profession over the past 10 years or so. However, I am aspirational. I am resilient. Despite the bombardment, political interference and the experience of redundancy, I am still here working with students and colleagues year in, year out. I consider myself to be a success and know that I still have years of lesson plans, assemblies and classroom ideas stored away in the engine room.

To be Vitruvian, you will need to be aspirational to survive, and also to step up!

#stickability

No matter what stage you are at in your career, it is important that you stay stuck in the classroom. Teaching is not for everybody, but it must be for you if you're reading this book. Our students need us, and so do our colleagues. If you have survived your formative years unscathed, you are a resilient soul. Now is the time to master the art of teacher intelligence, innovation and collaboration in order to be truly successful in one of the best and most necessary careers our society has.

It is crucial, that together we ignore the nonsense; we focus on teaching our subjects and our students well. We need to remind ourselves that teaching is so much more than imparting knowledge and subject skills in the classroom. We open doors. We provide each and every student with hopes and dreams. It is our duty to stay stuck in the classroom for as long as possible!

WHAT IS COVERED IN THIS SECTION?

In this section of the book, you will be reminded of what it takes to remain aspirational in challenging times:

- I discuss how you can continue to work smart, despite the changing curriculum, assessment and examination goalposts.

- I take you through a range of job roles you may encounter prior to taking up a role in middle leadership.

- I suggest ways to consider and reflect on what is required of you as you take a brave step up into middle leadership.

- I look at the challenges that aspiring teachers face, balancing the demands of an increased workload versus continued, high-quality classroom practice.

- And finally I look at how to manage a team, a department and other staff. It's all here. The Vitruvian teacher is almost complete!

Teaching is a wonderful career. Staying stuck in the classroom is a challenge, but the rewards await you once you master the art of classroom practice and develop your own pedagogy in a climate of heavy workload. If you can ignore the drivel and focus on what matters, then the step up towards middle and senior leadership – if that's what you are looking for – awaits you. Leadership is not for everyone, but the joys of leading others and supporting students across a larger community (beyond your classroom) are wonderful to behold. Be aspirational – success is what you make it!

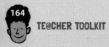

CLOSING THE GAP

'Closing the gap' – ensuring that all students make progress in all areas of school life.

Once you have started to secure consistently good teaching practice, you will probably be in a more informed position within your school. Your role will start to reach out beyond your own classroom – developing collaboration to a deeper level – and you will discover that you can address students who you may not directly teach day-to-day.

Firstly, here are my top strategies that I have tried and tested in my classroom over the past two decades. Most of the strategies can be used for all students and I would recommend that they are, but I've tried to be more specific and home in on classroom strategies I've used when differentiating for children from disadvantaged backgrounds over time. It's important, though, to find out what works in your school, for your students.

1. **Keep a rigorous track of your classroom data and use this to inform your lesson planning**

2. **If possible, communicate attainment regularly to students, particularly outside of whole school assessment deadlines** This will ensure that assessment becomes a normal routine in your classroom practice and learning environment. It goes without saying that regular feedback on progress, promotes self-evaluation and self-assessment.

3. **Create additional interventions for students who need it both inside and outside of the lesson** This could be something as simple as a 15 minute study club over lunch or after school with some alternative arrangements to entice the students to attend. Make it easier for yourself by focusing on just two to three children at a time.

4. **Communicate your plans to the students' pastoral leaders and every single parent/carer** You will need people around you to support you and your decisions, and for other people to collaborate when it comes to encouraging students to move forward.

5. **Seek support from specialised departments within the school** For example, EAL (English as an Additional Language) and SEN (Special Educational Needs) departments will have a raft of expertise in these faculty areas, so make sure you go and pick their brains. You may come across a couple of resource gems to support your plans. Even better, someone may volunteer their services!

6. **Seek specialist intervention where some emotional and/or behavioural intervention is needed** Most teachers do not have the expertise to work with students who need specialist intervention. If you think this additional support will help one or two key students to make progress in your own classroom, ask someone for advice.

7. **Look into recent programmes such as Aimhigher and The Brilliant Club** These are designed to widen participation in higher education by raising the aspirations of young people from disadvantaged groups. Challenging all students must start in your classroom and be a regular feature. You must teach to the top, all of the time, for all students. Be relentless!

THE MAIN AREAS WHERE YOU CAN MAKE A DIFFERENCE

In the rest of this chapter, I would like to suggest some effective classroom strategies for closing the gap for student achievement so that all students can be aspirational. The nature of this chapter would require another book in itself, but I just want to sow the seed when it comes to the range of students that you will teach in your own classroom and once you start to look outside your own four walls to students you may not teach.

PARENT/CARER INVOLVEMENT

Do all you can to get parents and carers on your side and involved with their child's education. Parental involvement is one of the most significant factors in raising students' attainment. The difficulty for most teachers, and for most schools, is that we all encounter hard to reach parents and carers, and this is particularly relevant to children from low-income families. Breaking habits with families with lower aspirations and apathy towards education is fundamental to a child's success. You cannot rely on one parents' evening every academic year. It's just not enough! Parent forums for specific groups, can have mixed, yet remarkable, success if structured correctly.

QUALITY OF TEACHING

It is the quality of teaching that makes the biggest difference to learning outcomes. As classroom practitioners we all know this – and we do not need international research evidence to tell us. Therefore your own pedagogy matters. Students with severe learning difficulties or barriers to their learning will need a good teacher who is determined, resolute and consistent in their approach to help close the gap with learning. It is vital for schools to coach teachers on using specific teaching methods and, in particular, strategies for the most vulnerable students. Simply changing how you deliver something and adapting schemes of work, in general do not produce large improvements in students' learning or necessarily close the gap. What

'ONE IN FOUR CHILDREN IN THE UK GROWS UP IN POVERTY AND FOR THESE CHILDREN THE IMPACT ON THE CLASSES OF EDUCATION AND LIFE SUCCESS IS PROFOUND. THE ATTAINMENT GAP BETWEEN CHILDREN FROM RICH AND POOR BACKGROUNDS IS DETECTABLE AT AN EARLY AGE (22 MONTHS)...'

Centre for Excellence and Outcomes in Children and Young People's Services

is required here, is that your interventions focus closely on the attainment gaps using a teaching repertoire that you know works.

TEAMWORK

No man is an island, and no teacher is either!

We cannot do this alone, and I would strongly recommend that you seek help from specialised teachers in your school. If you manage to find the elusive teaching assistant (see page 145) who is a regular feature in your classroom (much rarer in secondary schools), aim to have a planning meeting with them regularly so that you can pinpoint exactly which strategies and resources to use with individual students.

The most powerful methods for closing the achievement gap are produced through the use of well-supported teachers. How often have you been sent an IEP (Individual Education Plan) for a student and not spent enough time reading the details? This document will give you some ideas for learning/teaching strategies that could inform you of what your work with under-achieving students. And more often than not, they are not struggling; the door has just not been opened for them yet…

Some examples may include – and these may not be specific to your subject but just to get an idea – structured speaking and listening approaches when dealing with any literacy tasks, as well as a range of strategies for reading and writing in home and in target languages.

Although much of this support will come from one-to-one tutoring which you cannot do in a busy classroom, you can at least try some of the strategies promoted by the SEN/EAL departments in your school, and instruct students with bite-sized activities.

LANGUAGE AND LITERACY

> *'You can turn up hung-over every morning, wearing the same pair of creased Farahs as last week, with hair that looks like a bird has slept in it, then spend most of the lesson talking at kids about how wonderful you are; but mark their books with dedication and rigour and your class will fly!'* (@PhilBeadle, *How to Teach*)

Students' grasp of language and literacy skills during the early years in primary school is fundamental for them to access the curriculum and make good progress later on in their school life. Learning to read is the most important goal for all students, but in secondary school the focus shifts from reading to learning.It is vital that as teachers we develop a range of strategies in order to entice students to engage with their own literary demons.

CLOSE THE GAP

Instead of a rapid pace, try a slower pace. Instead of typical tasks such as completing various questions or paragraphs in an allocated time, try 'Slow Writing,' a writing technique suggested by David Didau in *The Secret of Literacy*. The tecnhique encourages students to slow down and 'approach each word, sentence and paragraph with love and attention.'

BEHAVIOUR FOR LEARNING

If you fail to follow your behaviour for learning policy, even with the most challenging students, then you are undermining your colleagues.

It is important to follow your behaviour for learning policy and ensure consistency in your own classroom and across the school. It is vital that if we want to raise standards of behaviour, close the gap and improve levels of literacy with the hardest of students, we must maintain a common language for discipline, literacy and student support across the school. Schools are no place for the maverick to go solo…

DIRECT INSTRUCTION

I am a huge fan of direct instruction. Although I'm not an expert in this particular pedagogy, I am an advocate for teacher clarity, or what I've become more and more used to describing as 'stickability'. Direct instruction is when a teacher provides instruction to students, focusing on a 'keep it simple' philosophy.

John Bayley (Teachers TV behaviour champion, @JohnBayley1) once said to me, and I have never forgotten it: 'Always focus on the primary behaviour'. This strategy can be applied to absolutely anything in the classroom. For example, instruction. Do not allow instructions to become unclear through distractions or random questions thrown out by students. Focus on what matters, focus on your instruction and what you have asked a student to do. This technique can never be underestimated when working with students who need that additional support.

ALTERNATIVE RESOURCES

It is important that students from disadvantaged backgrounds are integrated into the classroom environment like any other child.

Often, interventions may include the possibility of using alternative resources, but I would be reluctant to ostracise students in this way if they do not urgently require such additional resources. Only do this if they have a specific learning need that requires such resources to support learning. Instead, try using resources you already have in the room: the students! Use your seating plan and student data to place individual students alongside others who speak their language who can support and challenge their learning, or simply a classmate who makes them feel welcome in class. A happy student, is a student who learns best!

STUDENT SAFETY

How does a teacher get hold of the information they need to know in order to ensure that any child can be safe and in a position to learn? Teaching all of a sudden gets even more complicated, doesn't it? How would you feel, and what would you do if

you welcomed a vulnerable student to your tutor group or subject classroom? What background information should you receive before they arrive, and what should you do after their first lesson?

- **Safeguarding** It is essential for all new teachers – indeed every teacher – to be fully up to speed with safeguarding procedures and child protection in their school. This develops your resilience as a professional and not only allows you to protect and support a student, but also support yourself.

- **SEN** This is always a fascinating area of the school and full-time classroom teachers have little time available to truly understand what goes on in such specialist pockets of the school. Why not spend half a term regularly visiting the department to see what goes on? Speak with your SENCO; you will learn a vast amount about students and the challenging circumstances in which they live. Ask to receive regular updates.

Imagine a child has been diagnosed with a medical condition. They may have a SEN statement and allocated support provided. From the moment that child enters your classroom, you are dealing with a child that may require closer attention. Daily, weekly, monthly, every term? Communication will be vital between school and home or, in more desperate circumstances, with the police or social services. You and a few other colleagues may need specialist support or training and, if so, you definitely should have been informed prior to the student's arrival.

ASPIRATION TIP

The most powerful approach that you can take, is to keep your aspirations high. Refining your processes and teaching methods will deliver the greatest improvement in learning outcomes for children from disadvantaged backgrounds. You cannot do what you have always done. And this is particularly the case for students who need that extra little bit of support.

Think cognitively. Simply changing how you deliver something, whether this is through ICT or an approach to teaching a scheme of work, is much less effective. What will have the greatest impact on your students, is you. Schools who are successfully closing the gap support their staff in delivering good learning outcomes for all students. This requires an extensive and continuing professional development programme delivered within the school by experts from within. If you need help, go and speak with a colleague today, and do something about it!

MOVING ON IN YOUR CAREER

Who are you?
What do you do?
Where are you going?

These three simple and profound questions are the most difficult to answer professionally. Watch how often your answers and the reasoning behind them change over the years. This is a chapter about stepping up and moving on in your career; taking on more whole school responsibilities. It's time to be Vitruvian. It's time to get aspirational for yourself. So, what could you do next?

ADDITIONAL SCHOOL RESPONSIBILITIES

At some point in the formative years of your teaching career, whether you are looking for it or not, an additional role or responsibility will come your way. This may or may not be defined as promotion, and not quite on the cusp of whole school middle leadership, but it certainly could be a departmental or school responsibility.

ASPIRATION TIP

There is nothing wrong with setting your goals high in education, but make sure you are ready to be a leader of education. Whatever steps you take, it will no doubt force you to take one foot out of the classroom as the demands on your time focus more and more on working with other adults in your school, and sadly, less and less directly on students. To be aspirational is a good quality to possess, but make sure any decisions you make to be a leader of others are carefully calculated.

A wise man once said to me, 'If you are faced with a choice, always choose the more difficult of the two. This is the only way to grow.'

Additional school responsibilities

Second in department role

Coordinator roles
For example, ICT, gifted and talented, literacy, numeracy, etc.

Sports coordinator for events
For example, local community sports, sports day and fixtures.

NQT mentor
To run NQT sessions to help staff induction and colleagues settle into the school.

Enrichment coordinator
For example, DofE or activity week.

Mentoring and coaching
To support younger teachers new to the classroom.

Volunteer roles
Such as those designed to train teachers to then lead/ guide other teachers when introducing a new initiative, a piece of software, etc.

Transition manager
A point of contact between primary and secondary school.

Pastoral manager
For example, assistant heads of year to support student progress and behaviour.

Community links
Teachers working in their subjects with other schools/ Key Stages.

Librarian assistant
To support the work of the student resources; often to provide a presence to help maintain student etiquette and promote values of scholarship.

BEING A CHAMPION

In many schools there is the call for individuals to be 'champions' – to volunteer for additional unpaid roles; to represent their department and help steer a whole school project as part of a collaboration with somebody else.

Now, I am not discouraging you from doing this, because sometimes these voluntary roles are ideal for testing the waters, in terms of your own capacity to add additional workload on top of what you already do as a full-time class teacher. However, being a champion not only requires a level of expertise, knowledge or interest, but also attending meetings, completing paperwork and reporting information to and from departments. My advice would be:

- Volunteer for something that you are really interested in and do it well – rather than do nothing and be asked to be the representative for something you don't care about. If you are coerced into a role you are not passionate about, lay your cards on the table.

- Be clear about the commitment required.

I was once nominated for two additional roles that were not necessarily part of my day-to-day role; an unexpected responsibility as a middle leader. They were *Health and Safety representative* and the *STEM coordinator* for a whole school bid towards achieving specialist status in science. Both these demands fitted naturally with being Head of Design Technology, and when I looked left or right over my shoulders, there was nobody else but me who put their hand up.

Of course, as much as I loathed these additional (and not very interesting) tasks, looking back they did offer a degree of leadership knowledge to enable me to step up to senior leadership several years later. I learnt all about the intricacies of:

- managing meetings

- looking through agendas, minutes and tedious policies

- the art of delegation, nomination and tactful volunteering

- the art of collaboration

- refining my own aspirations.

All of these are essential skills for anyone taking on additional responsibilities that require the services of other colleagues.

WHEN TO MOVE UP THE LADDER

FIRST, A WARNING...

I firmly believe that you should master your classroom practice before you take on any additional roles within school. In many situations where I have worked, opportunities have arisen for colleagues for the wrong reasons.

WRONG REASONS

School circumstances

- There is nobody else available.
- The school needs to fill a vacancy.
- Somebody is off sick or on maternity leave and the role needs to be covered.

Personal circumstances

- Being promotion hungry.
- Motivated by money.
- Motivated by power.

Before taking on a new role in the school, ask yourself if any of the above personal reasons are the main purpose for taking on the role. Some of the circumstances may be contributing factors – that is OK (for example, a school vacancy coming up). But check with yourself before you commit.

WHAT IS THE MAIN REASON I WANT TO TAKE ON A NEW ROLE?

- Seeking new knowledge/challenge?
- A genuine vacancy and reason for applying?
- A stepping stone to the future?
- I am the right person for that job/school?

WHAT OTHER CONTRIBUTING REASONS MIGHT I HAVE FOR MAKING A CHANGE?

- Personal commitments with childcare?
- The journey to work?
- Difficult relationships with staff?
- Bored and need a new challenge?

'WHATEVER IT IS, BE GRATEFUL THAT YOU HAVE A JOB, AND THAT YOU ARE NOW IN A POSITION TO SEEK A NEW CHALLENGE.'

@TeacherToolkit

MIDDLE LEADERSHIP

This is a chapter about taking your professional life further by stepping up to middle leadership for the first time, and the possible roles you could embrace.

If you are successful as a classroom teacher, you are very likely to take on a middle leadership role within a school. Such a role is a form of whole school responsibility. You will be responsible for other staff and students and this is incredibly enriching, yet comes with high stakes! You are no longer flying solo, accountable only for your own classroom and your own results. Where once your head of department was your appraiser, you'll possibly now find that the head of faculty or a member of the senior leadership team is appraising you, and you are appraising others.

ASPIRING LEADERS

Ex-headteacher Jill Berry is a leader who has shared her support and challenge with me personally over the years, but also with countless others through her online presence. She has enabled me to aspire towards the dizzy heights of headship myself, enabling me to reflect on classroom practice and school leadership.

WHY WOULD ANYONE WANT TO BE LED BY YOU? @jillberry102

At a recent TeachMeet, former headteacher and current EdD student Jill Berry presented 'Why would anyone want to be led by you?' a speech about leadership for current and aspiring leaders. Her keynote question originates from Steve Munby, former chief executive of the National College for School Leadership, who is now chief executive of CfBT (Centre for British Teachers) Education Trust.

Berry asks: 'So, what is leadership all about? Well, leadership is incredibly complex, but also very simple. Leadership is about getting the best out of everyone you lead; really trying to get the best from each individual.'

You will face many challenges as a leader, and you may well be faced with leading individuals that you do not necessarily see eye to eye with! So, how will you get the best out of them? As Berry says, 'Some staff may be much less resilient or committed than you. They may be frightened of change, resistant, complacent, aggressive or argumentative. But you must never, ever give up on them when you become a leader and help them deal with their fears. You don't give up on them; you don't give up on anybody that you lead. Just as you don't give up on the children that you teach.'

Leadership is all about relationships and communication:

1. Are you the type of leader who pulls someone along with you?

2. Can you help people to feel calm, even in the toughest of times? Even if you are not feeling calm yourself? Can you still inspire trust and confidence in those you lead?

3. Can you create a sense of stability and safety even when the seas are very rough?

4. Do you have integrity? Can you cling to your core values, especially when they are tested?

5. Can you be positive and optimistic even when you are surrounded by unpalatable government initiatives and changes in policy you might or might not agree with?

6. And can you remember what it's all about? Can you remember what it was that brought you into teaching in the first place? That should still motivate you as a leader. Most people go into teaching because they want to make a difference to the lives of children. And this should be the same when you want to become a leader. Stepping up provides you with the opportunity to make more of a difference to the lives of your students and your colleagues.

7. Do not lose sight of what is really important.

Berry goes on to quote John Dunford, former general secretary of the Association of School and College Leaders (ASCL), who says all leaders should have the '4-Hs'.

1. Hope

2. Humanity

3. Humility

4. Humour

> 'ROUGH SEAS MAKE THE BEST SAILORS.'
> @jillberry102

Leaders need to be strong – to be able to hold colleagues to account; to be able to challenge them as well as support them – but they also need to be compassionate and humane. Leadership is who you are, it's not just about what you do.

Adapted from Jill Berry's presentation at TeachMeet London, 1st April 2015

MIDDLE LEADERSHIP ROLES

LEADING COLLEAGUES

As a young middle leader, I was so motivated being a head of department. When I look back, they were by far the most fulfilling years of teaching, without question! But why was I so happy? Well it was mainly to do with being more influential in terms of my own teaching practice and the impact I could have on other colleagues in a larger environment beyond my own classroom.

Here are my suggestions for the types of middle leadership role you might aspire to:

- leading on teaching and learning
- leading on your own professional development
- developing other staff
- dealing with other staff problems – whether this is holding other staff to account, or picking up the pieces when things go wrong
- understanding data
- having interventions and pathways in place

- being a subject specialist – the number one expert on knowledge, skills and understanding
- managing a budget
- developing your leadership style
- shaping the future
- developing yourself and working with others
- managing the organisation (or your sub-team)
- securing accountability.

LEADING TEACHING, LEARNING AND STUDENT PROGRESS

The fundamental roles for middle leaders – including support staff – are either working within the curriculum, or working pastorally and directly day-to-day with students. In either role you will soon understand, that timing is everything. When you're a middle leader, the importance of evaluative reviews or interventions with students is crucial to you and your team.

No matter what role you find yourself in, each role will relate directly back to:

- the quality of teaching and learning
- how well organised you are
- how you develop, monitor and evaluate an action plan.

THE GREATEST CHALLENGES FOR ANY MIDDLE LEADER

I consider the greatest challenges for any middle leader to be:

- balancing the friendships and the disagreements at a local level
- working as a team
- having a degree of accountability in

order to raise standards of teaching and learning for students and teachers within your remit

- keeping the quality of your own teaching as exemplary practice, despite balancing the challenges of increased workload middle leadership will bring.

FORWARD PLANNING

Forward planning is a crucial part of a middle leadership role, and you need to ask yourself the following questions:

1. **Timetable** Is the forthcoming timetable matched to the needs of the teachers, or the needs of the students?

2. **Plans** Have you reviewed your curriculum protocol plans currently on offer for each year group/Key Stage

3. **Schemes of work** What schemes of work are currently being monitored, evaluated, reviewed? By whom? By when?

4. **Observations** Can you use additional (non-contact) time you are allocated to complete triad (groups of three) observations with colleagues in your department?

5. **Teaching** How could you improve your own teaching? What needs to be refined?

6. **Personal development plan** What leadership skills are on your personal development plan? What are your areas for development?

7. **Feedback** On the surface, how does your department appear? What do the students say?

It's not going to be easy stepping up, but remember what Berry said: 'Rough seas make the best sailors.'

THE JOB HUNT

Over the past 20 years I've lost count of the number of applications I've submitted to various schools and the number of teachers I have interviewed myself.

In this chapter I will share my own 5 minute interview plan – devised after much deliberation about what I needed to do in order to secure a job – and then elaborate on finding a job, the interview process and of course the various scenarios that you may face, including the internal applicants dilemma.

THE 5 MINUTE INTERVIEW PLAN

- **Key facts** Are you clear what job you are looking for? Is the time right to apply for a job that you have seen advertised? If so, find out all the key facts about the job and what is required, and some information about the school so that you can decipher whether this is the right job for you. When is the deadline for the job application?

- **Person specification** Once your fact-finding mission is complete, you must now complete your application, addressing all the requirements in the person specification. Schools – or I should say very organised schools – are incredibly pedantic about this because they must adhere to equal opportunities, and have legal procedures to follow to ensure they are fulfilling their recruitment policy. If you do not address the person specification, it is highly unlikely that you will be shortlisted.

- **What can you offer the school?** Throughout your application, demonstrate that you have considered what you can offer to the school. Address this in your supporting statement, aligned to the person specification.

- **Key information** As you complete this exercise you will need to find out some key information, such as Grim Reaper information, and the school development plan if you can locate it. Perhaps look online to find some relevant data that best describes the context of the school and its overall performance. If you can gather this information, then you will demonstrate that you are working towards middle leadership.

- **Check it over** The following information is obvious, but you would be surprised how many applications have grammatical errors, crossings out and countless other horrors. Read and re-read your application until you're blue in the face, and then give it to someone else to read! Double-check that you have included your top priorities within your supporting statement, and check these against the person specification.

- **Supporting statement** My number one piece of advice would be to make the first paragraph in your supporting statement **draw the reader in so that they actually want to meet you in person!** Your application and work history will speak for themselves. Save the expansion of this detail for the interview. The shortlisting panel will make decisions based on the information you have accumulated over your education and career. But your statement and the quality of your written application can often be the tipping point. Getting in the door will give you the chance to elaborate and pick up on key points the panel may find pertinent.

5 MINUTE INTERVIEW PLAN

…photocopy or download, and scribble your way to a new job!

START
5:00

JOB ADVERT – THE KEY FACTS

PERSON SPECIFICATION

THE DAY BEFORE

THE TOP 5 PRIORITIES IN MY SUPPORTING STATEMENT ARE:

1
2
3

WHY SHOULD I WORK HERE?

SCHOOL

WHAT DO I NEED TO FIND OUT?

?

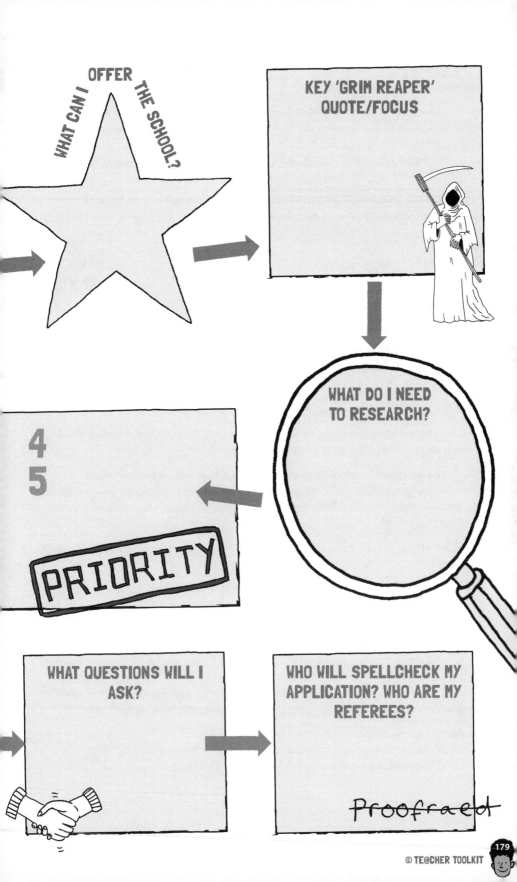

WHAT CAN I OFFER THE SCHOOL?

KEY 'GRIM REAPER' QUOTE/FOCUS

WHAT DO I NEED TO RESEARCH?

4
5

PRIORITY

WHAT QUESTIONS WILL I ASK?

WHO WILL SPELLCHECK MY APPLICATION? WHO ARE MY REFEREES?

Proofraed

THE INTERVIEW

Do not pin all your hopes on this interview. It will backfire on you. My best approach has always been to use the process as a professional development exercise. If you treat an interview as a training opportunity, then you will enjoy the experience much, much more and you will probably come across more confidently; possibly even secure the job! (I know, I've managed it seven times!)

In all instances, if you are asked to attend an interview, you truly do have one foot already in the door. It's time to calculate your next step...

Toolkit essential: preparing for an interview

- Plan well ahead, before the day of your interview.

- Arrive incredibly early. You can never be punished for being early, but you can certainly be punished for being late. There is absolutely no harm in overcompensating for this.

- Think about why you should work in that school, just in case you are asked.

- Be mindful that a panel might ask you what your areas for development are, so you will need to consider this very carefully.

- On the day itself, think about the information that you need to find out – not necessarily just during the interview, but also on the school tour when talking with students, meeting with colleagues and particularly when you are free to roam around the school.

- Think ahead to when you are free to roam around the school. Where will you go first? What information will help you in your interview?

- What questions can you ask, and is it important that you do ask them (or not)? Don't feel for one moment that you need to ask questions in order to show off, but it's a good idea to have at least one question prepared.

- Be prepared – I have attended two job interviews where I was given just over one day to prepare. I managed to secure one of the jobs! In most cases, you will be given plenty of notice. So, you will have plenty of time to prepare what you are going to wear and plan for your interview and your lesson observation and any other aspects of the process, for example a portfolio or presentation.

- Sleep – no matter whether you have a one- or a two-day process, get to bed early! You'd be surprised how obvious this is the very next day between candidates sitting on the other side of the table.

From application to interview

1. **Research online.** Use social media for research and support. Consider visiting the school.

2. **Plan your application** and ensure you have all the necessary components that have been requested.

3. **Speak to people.** Speak with your own colleagues as well as your future employers if you are unsure about anything.

4. **Take time over your application.** Spend a considerable amount of time completing the application. Once you have finished it and are failing to see the wood for the trees, take a step back and allow someone else to proofread it.

5. **Proofread and spellcheck** and proofread and spellcheck some more.

6. **Do not miss the deadline!**

7. **Wait patiently.** Do not call the school. If you are shortlisted you will be told – so long as you have filled in the correct email address and contact telephone number.

8. **You are shortlisted!** Hurray!

9. **Complete a test journey to the school.** Plan your route, what you are going to wear and what you will eat for breakfast. Might seem silly, but vital preparation.

10. **Be prepared.** Check your journey arrangements, your outfit and essentials: phone, wallet, keys, portfolio, etc.

11. **Go to bed early.** Set two alarms calls.

12. **Leave the house very early!** Arrive in your smartest outfit and enjoy the process. Smile and offer a firm handshake. Listen to names carefully and establish eye contact at every opportunity...

THE INTERNAL CANDIDATE DICHOTOMY

TWISTED-STOMACH SENSATION!

You're on parade in front of all your colleagues and teaching your own students for a job that you've probably already been doing! Yet you still might not secure the job.

HEART SINKS!

You arrive and find out that there is an internal candidate who will know much more about the school than you do!

Having been on both sides of this I can affirm that the interview process is truly about the performance on the day of the most suitable (not best) candidate who can secure the job. It is all about the teacher matching the person specification and the appointing panel being fair in their appointment process. Sadly, it may sometimes be based on a one-off performance.

STAR MODEL FOR INTERVIEW QUESTIONS

Contributed by Sapuran Gill, @ssgill76

Situation

Task ➡️ Set the context for your answer.

Action ➡️ Explain what you did, how you did it and why.

Results ➡️ Describe what you accomplished and what you learnt.

Twitter name? @kennypieper

Name in real life? Kenny Pieper

What's his job? Classroom teacher

Specialist topic? An English teacher in Scotland who blogs plenty of book reviews and advocates on his blog that he is 'only trying to be better than yesterday'. That's a good philosophy in my opinion!

Why should I follow him? Pieper blogs here at: http://justtryingtobebetter.net. He is also the curator of Pedagoo, a growing community of teachers collaboratively supporting, encouraging and sharing innovative and effective approaches to education. Check out his webiste: http://pedagoo.org

AFTER THE INTERVIEW

YOU'VE BEEN APPOINTED! WHAT NEXT?

1. Congratulations! Go and celebrate; these are rare events!

2. Slow down! You have a job that you need to finish.

3. Prepare a handover list for the person (if applicable) who will be taking over your role/classes/tutor group, etc.

4. Start thinking about the 'big things' you need to do before you leave your current school, such as packing; recycling; preparing to move; saying your goodbyes.

5. Start preparing for your new job. You are entitled to have one day (paid – but do check, and also ask if you can go!) visiting your new school.

6. Prepare a simple 'what do I need?' list. Remember, the staff you are visiting in your new school will be busy and definitely not as excited as you are. Plan for time to meet with key staff.

7. Take some time out to rest before you move school – usually it will coincide with a school holiday.

8. Go slow. Listen. Listen for a long time. Support… and then challenge.

YOU'VE BEEN UNSUCCESSFUL! WHAT NEXT?

1. Chin up! It will happen in good time.

2. Seek detailed feedback from the panel. Arrange a quiet place to write key points down.

3. It's your entitlement to be offered feedback. The best schools will make you feel that: a) you've left with great developmental feedback; b) you still want to work there. The ripple (word-of-mouth) effect can travel miles!

4. Get back to your day job quickly. Don't mope around. It wasn't your time.

5. Consolidate any action points and feedback from the interview. Discuss them with your line manager/mentor and work to address key issues.

6. Research new job adverts. Take your time. Don't apply for everything!

7. Work hard on the next application. Don't change anything too radical. Be yourself.

8. Stay hungry for the job. Turn that hunger into passion, not desperation. Become all that is Vitruvian: Resilient; Intelligent; Innovative; Collaborative and Aspirational.

ASPIRATION TIP

It is important to live the job you want, but do not overcook the idea. If you are truly in a good position for securing a new job, you should have already been testing the boundaries in your current position; shadowing colleagues and speaking with others who have been offering support and challenge.

Network with colleagues, keep your eye on the job market and be fussy about what you apply for. Oh, and my final piece of advice is this: only apply for a job when you are personally in a strong place.

BUILDING A DEPARTMENT

'Challenge: here's £50,000 to design a new set of classrooms and a department.'

What are you going to do, and why? How are you going to spend it? How are you going to justify your decisions to your headteacher? This chapter is about designing and building a department – metaphorically and physically. (See section 4 for tips on working with colleagues as you build your department.)

I was in a very fortunate position as a new middle leader to be tasked with building a department in a brand new school. There were absolutely no facilities, and the new school was operating in a former college building that was due for demolition, construction then partial refurbishment. Even if you are not lucky enough to do this, this advice will apply to all new middle leaders.

During the eight years I worked in this department, I rebuilt the department three times as each area of the school was built, recamped, demolished and rebuilt. As a guesstimate, I must have been responsible for spending £500, 000 on equipment, machinery and, eventually, stationery. It was incredibly exciting and challenging knowing that the decisions I made on infrastructure and machinery, would potentially last 25 years or more! As I write this chapter now, the department I set up still exists today, almost 15 years later.

I learnt many lessons throughout the process, and in this chapter I would like to offer some thoughts and advice for you to ponder. The issues you should consider are:

- expenditure and budget
- health and safety
- planning permission
- dealing with architects
- student movement
- fixtures, fittings and furniture
- choices – things to keep/ throw away
- snagging lists.

BEFORE YOU BEGIN...

There are two key points you must consider before starting out:

The school's ethos and mission statement

Where is the school going? What does it want to achieve for every single student that passes through it?

Your vision and values

What are your personal vision and values for your own classroom(s) and department? Becoming a leader is what you are, it's not just about what you do.

'YOU HAVE TO KNOW WHAT YOU WANT YOUR SCHOOL TO LOOK LIKE. HAVE A VISION READY TO COMMUNICATE TO ALL STAFF, PARENTS AND STUDENTS.'
Potential headship advice: Stephen Drew (@StephenDrew72), December 2012, SLTeachMeet

1. EXPENDITURE AND BUDGET

OK, you need to design a new classroom and have £50,000. What are you going to do first?

- Basic furniture such as tables and chairs is going to cost almost £15,000.

- Pens, stationery and exercise books for all year groups to pass through your classroom door for one academic year will cost approximately £5,000.

You have £30,000 left. What are you going to do?

This will vary from subject to subject and with area of responsibility. You currently have an empty classroom full of tables and chairs and a stockpile of stationery. There is nothing else, apart from windows and a door.

MY TOP 5 PURCHASES FOR A CLASSROOM

1.

2.

3.

4.

5.

(Tweet image to @TeacherToolkit)

2. HEALTH AND SAFETY

You have a planning meeting with the architect and your headteacher and discover that certain doors, windows (or machinery if you work in a practical subject) have, for health and safety reasons, been planned in the wrong positions! Unfortunately, there are no options other than to move some of these items to a new location before the start of the academic year. The deduction from your own budget is £10,000. You are incredibly frustrated!

What would you do? How would you deal with this? What decisions would you have to change? How would you communicate this to your team? How would you feed back to your headteacher once you had calmed down?

3. PLANNING PERMISSION

My advice, as a classroom teacher and a middle leader, is that you don't really need to know much about this at this stage of

your career and I wouldn't worry about this unless it is vital to your build.

However, it's a fascinating world and if you are ever involved in a brand-new building, you may be required to understand some planning regulations in order to meet certain design decisions. For example, the positioning of the classroom door, air extraction or height of the electricity outlets. This is particularly the case for leadership teams working on project builds with construction companies.

4. DEALING WITH ARCHITECTS

Of all the architects I have worked with over the past 20 years, I've never met one that has been a teacher. They will all tell you that they have worked in hundreds of schools and understand the needs of the teachers, but unfortunately the effect of adding the 1,500 students into the building never lives up to the architect's vision of how the building will work day-to-day.

It is therefore important that you spend a great deal of time getting involved in any planning stage to make critical decisions. It's up to you as a teacher to spot the potential snags – for example, the cupboard, light or entrance being in the wrong position – which will make that particular space more congested than it needs to be.

These simple decisions are crucial for your own and your students' well-being. It will affect the behaviour of your students, so the psychology of the design is equally important as the design decisions.

5. STUDENT MOVEMENT

For a generation, schools have been poorly designed and thousands of teachers have struggled to teach in dilapidated environments. Thankfully, recent government projects and funding have given schools a new lease of life and improved student flow. This is not only in the classroom, but the outside areas have become quite a significant factor in supporting the ethos of the school and the learning of each student. As a result, behaviour and motivation should improve.

With this in mind, if you are lucky enough to redesign the classroom or design your own department, think carefully about:

- the flow of traffic
- where students sit to complete their work
- where they will complete practical activities
- where you (the teacher) will be positioned in all of this.

Don't forget the last simple consideration that every teacher can control – your desk! I've walked into so many classrooms, only to see the teacher working away at their desk, facing away from the students, with the table pushed up against the wall. If yours looks like this, turn it around immediately! It is so important to face the students when you are working at your desk during the lesson.

6. FIXTURES, FITTINGS AND FURNITURE

The small details can make all the difference. Don't underestimate the importance of where the light switch is, the door knob or which way the door opens in your classroom.

Getting it right leads to happier teachers and students, which equates to more productive lessons. Much of this detail will be out of your hands, but if you're lucky enough to design your own classroom, make sure you have a careful think about what you need and how you can influence the decisions made.

7. CHOICES

For my Masters degree in design, one project asked us to focus on the psychology of colours. It opened up a whole new world for me; a world I explored in the classroom. I have fond memories of the purple food technology classroom I designed. Looking back, it was colourful!

There is a great deal of academic research on colours in education. For example, colours are incredibly important in the early stages of child development. This focus should never be lost in schools. Sadly many secondary schools move towards bland and corporate colours for marketing purposes; often to match a very traditional uniform constrained by the awful range of colours provided by the uniform suppliers! Thankfully many school leaders can see the importance of having fresh, bright, open and airy spaces to inspire students and their learning.

8. SNAGGING LISTS

In my current role (at the time of writing), we were given the set of keys to move into a new building at 5pm on a Friday before students were due to arrive the following Monday morning! There were still over 4,000 outstanding issues to be resolved. Three months later, and as I write this now, there are still over 1,000 issues to be resolved. These issues can vary in length and depth of work. For example, installing a handrail to provide additional safety to students, excavating the surface and reinstalling plumbing and pipework underneath the floors to toilets that were not working correctly. The list goes on…

Every school will have someone in charge of this list. It is important that your jobs are on this list as a middle leader and that you keep a close track of the work to be completed. Take photographs and communicate issues regularly, including the jobs that are incomplete or not up to standard, to your line manager and to the appropriate people concerned.

ASPIRATION TIP

It doesn't matter if you never get the chance to work in a new building throughout your career. Although I had the opportunity to redesign several classrooms in my third year of teaching, I had never worked in a new school build until my 20th year! Regardless of what opportunities may come your way, it is vital to remain aspirational when working in any school building. Not just for yourself and your own motivation when turning up to work, but also for wanting the best for your students and the facilities in which they are learning.

MANAGING OTHER STAFF

Think about all the line managers you have had as a teacher. Who inspired you? Who didn't, and why? What has led you to become a middle leader? How will you support and challenge colleagues working in your department?

Leadership is incredibly rewarding and equally demanding. In the Vitruvian style, your job is never done and you will be accountable to those who work for you. This is a chapter about being truly aspirational as you take that step towards managing other staff. In this chapter I will focus on what makes a good middle leader, line management, appraisal and having that all-important difficult conversation.

TAKE A LOOK AT YOURSELF

Before thinking about managing others, think about yourself. Consider completing a 360-degree self-review of your leadership and management style, and aim to do this with a critical friend. Remember all the bad experiences you have had with various line managers? How are you going to ensure that you avoid making the same mistakes with staff working for you?!

To a degree, all middle leaders should know about self-evaluation, earned autonomy and strategies for school improvement. After all, you will be the project manager for planning and implementing the change in your team area. At times, you may need to create policy through consultation and review, with informed decision-making matched against strict and strategic financial planning. As a middle leader, I was responsible for the management of our departmental budget of about £10,000–15,000 per annum. It would have been incredibly easy to make poor choices!

You will also need to develop your own strategies for handling performance management and personnel issues in your own team. You will need to be able to think creatively to anticipate and solve problems. And although much of this sounds like what you are used to as a teacher, it's a whole new level to be able to master.

LINE MANAGEMENT

Be honest, fair and transparent!

I have always enjoyed being a line manager. I would never say I'm the greatest teacher/leader to work with or for, but I do consider myself to be honest, fair and transparent in the relationship. If you can lead by these principles, even when dealing with difficult situations, you will always ensure that you are meeting the needs of your students.

What makes a good middle leader?

Able to make informed decisions

Motivated

Can think creatively to anticipate and solve problems

Incredibly reflective

Sets up effective systems and structures

Able to delegate where appropriate

#ASPIRATIONAL

#RESILIENT

LESSON PLANS

#COLLABORATIVE

#INTELLIGENT

#INNOVATIVE

Knows they still have things to learn

Organised

Has whole school improvement in mind

Excellent at collaborating with others

Sets realistic workloads for colleagues

Able to prioritise

Professional

APPRAISAL

Appraisal should be a supportive and developmental process designed to ensure that all staff have the skills and help they need to carry out their role effectively. The process should be open, transparent and fair, based on evidence and equal opportunities. If done well, it can show an indication of robust and supportive systems and structures in place across the school. As a leader, you will have to line-manage others and ensure that you are firstly following the school policy, but secondly and most importantly that you are not only holding a member of staff to account, but supporting them well in order for them to develop professionally. This is a very fine line to tread.

MANAGING DIFFICULT CONVERSATIONS

It is part and parcel of a school leader's job, that they will at some point face a difficult conversation where they must take action.

Whatever the circumstances, these conversations never stop being difficult, but leaders should always work hard on making them easier. Prior to promotion, no middle leader has ever really had any formal training for managing difficult conversations. So the process is incredibly important to get right.

For difficult conversations to be handled sufficiently, conversations must start with the students and the job. If the job is not being done, the students are suffering. If it starts with the member of staff, then the conversation may become a 'person/personality' issue and not the task/job/role being conducted to the desired standard.

> 'THERE ARE TWO MATTERS WHEN IT COMES TO TRICKY STAFFING ISSUES: THEY EITHER CAN'T DO IT, OR THEY WON'T DO IT. IF IT'S THE FORMER, THEN ITS A MATTER OF CAPABILITY; PERHAPS A NEED FOR TRAINING (OR AN IMPROVED APPRAISAL PROCESS ON THE PART OF THE LEADER). IF IT'S THE LATTER, THEN IT WILL BE A DISCIPLINARY ISSUE. WE NEED THIS DONE PROPERLY, BECAUSE OTHERWISE THE STUDENTS WILL SUFFER.'
>
> Paul Sutton, OBE (Greig City Academy)

Toolkit essential: managing difficult conversations

1. **Have the conversation sooner rather than later** Too often we postpone the difficult conversation because we know that it won't be easy and will potentially drain our own energies and emotions. While it is important not to rush into something, procrastination simply makes the situation worse. Keep the matter private, professional and germane.

2. **Stick to the facts** Describe carefully the behaviour that has led you to speak to the individual. Have all the facts ready. Describe the impact of the behaviour on others. For example, students, fellow colleagues or yourself, but be clear on the distinction between reality and perception. Ensure the person understands why there has to be a change in behaviour. Always have to hand the Teachers' Standards and your own school policies. If you do need to quote from them, allow adequate time for the individual to read the details before responding. Hopefully, this level of detail will not be needed, as an initial conversation is often all that is required to rectify most situations.

3. **Focus on the future** Talk about what is going to be different in the future. Depending on the nature of the conversation, this could be specific procedures that are required to be put into place, or simply a verbal commitment from the individual to take what has been said and act on it.

4. **Show respect** No matter how important the issue is, always ensure that you show respect for the individual as a person. You are taking issue only with the behaviours and not the individual. Give the member of staff time to digest, respond and reflect.

5. **Allow time** Even where the issue is perfectly clear and must be addressed, ensure the individual's voice is heard. While you are dealing with a particular issue, you are also modelling a process that shows respect for all.

6. **Keep a tight control of your emotions** Don't allow your emotions to get the better of you. To raise justifiable concerns in an unjustifiable manner simply creates more problems. Always be professional, and remember that they are not enjoying this either!

7. **Reflect** After the event, always reflect on how you could have done better, and then move on. Beware of replaying conversations again and again in your head; what you should have said or not said. This can be exhausting. Accept what is done and move on. Sometimes a small follow-up conversation or nod of the head is enough when next seeing or meeting with the same colleague.

WHAT WOULD YOU DO?
Tweet me @TeacherToolkit

ASPIRATION TIP

Think about what you expect from your own appraiser. What's missing and what needs doing? Are they managing the paperwork? Are you? Are they supporting and challenging you; setting, agreeing and negotiating targets and tasks? Apply that feedback to yourself as the appraiser.

Work on building your appraiser/appraisee relationship together. Find out what motivates them professionally and what their interests are personally. Consider having your meetings in a different location, away from your domain and in a neutral space, or even in their classroom or office. Sit far away from any computer and focus on recording any actions (only). Focus on them, maintain eye contact, listen and listen well.

And finally

This book is the result of my lifelong love of teaching; from trainee teacher to middle leader, from the helm of senior leadership to the brink of headship. Great teaching isn't complicated; it's about getting the simple things right and Vitruvian Teaching is about staying in the classroom and surviving beyond the time publicised in the attrition statistics. What we need to do is to support each other, especially new teachers joining the profession to help them to stay 'stuck' in the job. This will only come about through genuine investment in teacher training before and during our careers. As well as that, I believe the five attributes of great teaching explored in this book will arm new teachers with the skills they need to survive.

If you have made it to year 5 and have chosen to stay in the classroom you too can now move on to shape thousands of lives. TE@CHER TOOLKIT is an exploration of teaching at the heart of a classroom near you. I hope it is yours!

Welcome to Vitruvian teaching and to one of the best jobs in the world! Tweet me your thoughts using #VitruvianTeaching

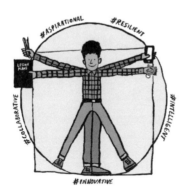

I told you I wouldn't mention the 'O' word, didn't I?

BIBLIOGRAPHY

ATL PPA Guidance: www.atl.org.uk/help-and-advice/workload-and-hours/ppa-time.asp

BBC 'Two-thirds of teachers feel undervalued, says OECD study': http://www.bbc.co.uk/news/business-27985795

Beadle, P. (2010–), How to Teach (series). Bancyfelin: Crown House Publishing

Berger, R 'Austin's Butterfly': www.youtube.com/watch?v=PZo2PIhnmNY

Berry, J 'Why would anyone want to be led by you?': Presentation at TeachMeet London, 1st April 2015

Blatchford, R. 'Thoughts on lesson observations #1: The surgeon and the scalpel': nationaleducationtrustblog.wordpress.com/2015/04/19/thoughts-on-lesson-observations-1-the-surgeon-and-the-scalpel/

British Library 'Vitruvius's theory of beauty', www.bl.uk/learning/artimages/bodies/vitruvius/proportion.html)

Clarke, P. 'Report into allegations concerning Birmingham schools arising from the "Trojan Horse" letter' © Crown copyright 2014: www.gov.uk/government/publications/birmingham-schools-education-commissioners-report

Centre for Excellence and Outcomes in Children and Young People's Services. 'Effective classroom strategies for closing the gap in educational achievement for children and young people living in poverty, including white working-class boys':

http://archive.c4eo.org.uk/pdfs/3/Schools%20and%20Communities%20RR%20P4.pdf

Concise Oxford English Dictionary (12th edition). Oxford: Oxford University Press

Creasy, M. (2014), Unhomework. Bancyfelin: Independent Thinking Press

DfE 'A profile of teachers in England from the 2010 school workforce census': www.gov.uk/government/uploads/system/uploads/attachment_data/file/182407/DFE-RR151.pdf

DfE 'Keeping children safe in education': www.gov.uk/government/publications/keeping-children-safe-in-education--2

DfE and Education Funding Agency: 'Pupil premium: funding and accountability for schools': www.gov.uk/

pupil-premium-information-for-schools-and-alternative-provision-settings

DfE 'School census: guide to submitting data': www.gov.uk/school-census

DfE 'School discipline and exclusions': www.gov.uk/school-discipline-exclusions/discipline

DfE 'Teachers' standards': www.gov.uk/government/publications/teachers-standards

DfE 'Workload challenge: analysis of teacher responses': www.gov.uk/government/publications/workload-challenge-analysis-of-teacher-responses

Didau, D. (2014), *The Secret of Literacy*. Bancyfelin: Crown House Publishing

Dix, P. '40 tips for NQTs': www.pivotaleducation.com/40-tips-for-nqts

Dix, P. 'Right you are in detention... er... next Thursday: Delayed sanctions have less impact': www.pivotaleducation.com/right-you-are-in-detention-er-next-thursday-delayed-sanctions-have-less-impact/#sthash.HxqOStFm.dpuf

Drabble, C. 'Letter to Mr Gove re teaching assistants. Please RT': cherrylkd.wordpress.com/2013/06/08/letter-to-mr-gove-re-teaching-assistants-please-rt/

Dweck, C. TED talks The power of believing that you can improve:

www.ted.com/talks/carol_dweck_the_power_of_believing_that_you_can_improve?language=en

Education Endowment Foundation 'Making Best Use of Teaching Assistants':

educationendowmentfoundation.org.uk/news/teaching-assistants-should-not-be-substitute-teachers-but-can-make-a-real-d/

Groome, D. (2014), *An Introduction to Cognitive Psychology, Processes and Disorders* (3rd ed.). Hove: Psychology Press

Kidd, D. (2014), *Teaching: Notes from the Front Line*. Bancyfelin: Independent Thinking Press

NASUWT teachers' satisfaction and well-being in the workplace survey: www.comres.co.uk/polls/nasuwt-teachers-satisfaction-and-wellbeing-in-the-workplace-survey

NEN Copy Rights and Wrongs 'Schools and Copyright': www.copyrightsandwrongs.nen.gov.uk/

NTEN 'What is Lesson Study?': http://tdtrust.org/nten/lesson-study/what-is-ls/

O'Leary, M. (2014), *Classroom Observation: A Guide to the Effective Observation of Teaching and Learning*. London: Routledge

O'Leary, M. 'Teachers and lesson observations': http://teachertoolkit.me/2014/09/10/teachers-and-lesson-observations-by-drmattoleary/

Pierson, R. 'Everybody needs a champion', TED Talks Education: www.ted.com/talks/rita_pierson_every_kid_needs_a_champion?language=en

Roberts, H. (2012), *Oops!*. Bancyfelin: Independent Thinking Press

School Teachers' Pay and Conditions Document: www.gov.uk/government/publications/school-teachers-pay-and-conditions-2014

Sherrington, T. 'Authentic assessment and progress: keeping it real': http://headguruteacher.com/2014/10/19/authentic-assessment-and-progress-keeping-it-real/

TES Professional.'How maverick teachers ruin behaviour management for everybody else': www.tes.co.uk/news/school-news/tes-professional/how-maverick-teachers-ruin-behaviour-management-everybody-else

Teacher Development Trust 'Developing Great Teaching': tdtrust.org/wp-content/uploads/2015/06/Developing-Great-Teaching-Summary.pdf

'Self-regulation' www.toolsofthemind.org/philosophy/self-regulation

Wiliam, D. 'Principled curriculum design': www.ssatuk.co.uk/wp-content/uploads/2013/09/Dylan-Wiliam-Principled-curriculum-design-chapter-1.pdf

Wiliam, D. 'Teacher quality: why it matters, and how to get more of it': http://www.dylanwiliam.org/Dylan_Wiliams_website/Papers.html

Note: I have tried my best to carefully reference all of the ideas I mention in this book, but due to the fantastic world of sharing resources online there may be an idea, strategy or utterance that I have not referenced correctly. If this is the case please do contact me and I will rectify!

INDEX

D

E

F

G

H

I

J

K

L